ᴛʜᴇREP

y Theatre

re

ᵦy Kaite O'Reilly

First performance
The Door
Birmingham Repertory Theatre
30 November 2000

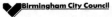

Providing Theatre for Birmingham

EUROPEAN COMMUNITY

European Regional
Development Fund

Artistic Director
Bill Alexander

Executive Producer
John Stalker

Associate Artistic Director
Anthony Clark

Associate Director
Indhu Rubasingham

Birmingham Repertory Theatre
Broad Street, Birmingham B1 2EP

Administration 0121 245 2000
Facsimile 0121 245 2100
Box Office 0121 236 4455

Notes when writing *Belonging*
by Kaite O'Reilly

In this age of fast and cheap air travel, the 'global village' and multi-cultural societies - is the issue of 'Belonging' to any one place outdated? Why does immigration, for some, still feel like exile? Can you feel homesick for a place you've never lived?

These and other questions confronted me when I chose to write about the complex relationship between the English West Midlands and its Irish Community.

Growing up Irish in Birmingham in the 1970's was a formative and defining experience. I'm sure like many immigrants from other parts of the world I was constantly aware of my duality - English in Ireland and Irish in England - yet this identity was further complicated by the effects of the IRA bombing campaign, when a war was carried out - literally - on our doorstep.

In *Belonging* I wanted to explore our diverse and sometimes troubled shared history and to celebrate a city and its people as we grow into the twenty-first century together.

Kaite O'Reilly
September 2000

With thanks to Ann and Malcolm Rose, Sam Boardman-Jacobs, Bill Hopkinson,Phillip Zarrilli and to Edmund McAuley for Finnigan the leprechaun.

Belonging
by Kaite O'Reilly

Production Credits

For *The Slight Witch*
Asda, Small Heath
Van den Bergh Foods
G Bates, Gunsmiths
Thermos Flasks
Aladdin
Burton's Biscuits
Jacob's Bakery
Sherwoods
Express Dairies
The Fishing Lodge
Boots the Chemist, Broad Street

For *A Wedding Story*
Alpha Travel Retail
Hyatt Hotel
Tyco Healthcare
Tridias Toys
Wedgewood
John Bull, Best of British
Winspers Florists
Liz Bolton PR
Farmfoods
Veuve Clicquot (UK) Ltd
Luminarc
Timex Watches
Kendal Continence Care
Carlton

For *Belonging*
Robert's Radio
Swedish Match
Goodmans
Let's Party
Jacob's Bakery
The Old Bushmills Distillery Co.
Guinness

Maura
Eileen Pollock

Fergal
John O'Mahony

Aine
Jacqui O'Hanlon

Seaneen
Iain McKee

Billy
James Hayes

Speaker
Niamh Linehan

Director
Anthony Clark

Designer
Rachel Blues

Lighting Designer
Symon Harner

Sound
Dean Whiskens

Stage Manager
Niki Ewen

Deputy Stage Manager
Clare Loxley

Assistant Stage Manager
Siobhan O'Neill

Biographies

THEREP

James Hayes
Billy

Trained: Guildhall
School of Music
and Drama

Recent theatre includes: Polonius
in *Hamlet*; Joyless in *The Antipodes*
(Shakespeare's Globe); *Tear From
A Glass Eye* (Gate Theatre); *Lenny*
(Queens).

For the National Theatre at the Old
Vic: *Richard II*; *As You Like It*; *The
White Devil*; *The Good Natured Man*;
Macbeth; *The Front Page*; *The
Misanthrope*; *Grand Manoeuvres*. More
recently
at the RNT: *Galileo*; *The Romans in
Britain*; *Amadeus*; *Strider*; *The Spanish
Tragedy*; *As I Lay Dying*; *Coriolanus*;
The Fawn; *The Orestia*; *A Chorus of
Disapproval*; *A View From The Bridge*;
Othello. For the RSC: *The Tempest*;
Elgar's Rondo; *The Venetian Twins*;
The Hostage; *The Taming Of The
Shrew*; *Faust*; *Woyzeck*; *The Cherry
Orchard*; *The Lion The Witch And The
Wardrobe*; *The Winter's Tale*. Also,
Faith Hope And Charity (Lyric
Hammersmith); *The Beaux Stratagem*
(Cambridge Theatre);
The Rules Of The Game (Albery);
A View From The Bridge (Aldwych). UK
Tour: *Whose Life Is It Anyway*; World
Tours (ESC): *The Winter's Tale*;
Coriolanus; *Macbeth*; *Twelfth Night*.

Wrote and performed two one-man
shows at the RNT: *Russell Of The
Times* and *A Horde Of Unemployed
Ventriloquists*.

TV: *Colditz*; *Tiptoe Through The Tulips*;
Red Roses For Me; *The Professionals*;
Emmerdale; *You're On Your Own*; *Hold
The Dream*; *On The Shelf*; *A Bunch of
Fives*; *The Orestia*; *Howard's Way*;
Bergerac; *The March*; *The Piglet Files*;
Parnell; *Wild Justice*; *A Question of
Guilt*; *Jacob*; *A Touch Of Frost*; *The Bill*.

Recent Radio: Wrote *Picture This*
(RTE); *The Troy Trilogy*.

Niamh Linehan
Speaker

For Birmingham
Repertory Theatre
Company: Pegeen
in *Playboy Of The
Western World*.

Theatre: Masha in *The Seagull* (RSC);
Aksyusha in *The Forest* (Royal National
Theatre); Portia in *The Merchant of
Venice* (Sheffield Crucible); Kathleen in
Long Days Journey Into Night (Plymouth
& Young Vic); *Dancing at Lughnasa*
(Lyceum, Edinburgh); *Top Girls*, *Habeus
Corpus* (Salisbury Rep); *The Government
Inspector* (Tricycle Theatre). European
tour of three plays by Howard Barker
and many productions with the major
companies of Ireland with leading roles
in *A Midsummer Nights Dream*; *Othello*;
Much Ado About Nothing and *Simpatico*
(nominated Best Actress, Irish Theatre
Awards 1998).

TV: *The Bill*

Radio: *A World Full of Weeping, Peels
Brimstone* (BBC Radio 4); *Riverun,
Monica Moody Show* (RTE).

Film: *The General*; *Niamh and the Angels*.

Iain McKee
Seaneen

Trained:
Rose Bruford
College.

Theatre: *The Northern Trawl*
(Hull Truck Theatre); *Masterclass*
(Bath Theatre Royal and Tour);
Early Morning (Royal National
Theatre Studio).

TV: *Cops* (World Productions).

Film: *The Bunker; The Parole Officer;
24 Hours After My Last Death;
Distasteful*.

Jacqueline O'Hanlon
Aine

Trained: University of Birmingham

For Birmingham Repertory Theatre
Company: Corrie Fox in *Mohicans*.

Theatre: Hermia in *A Midsummer
Night's Dream* (London Bubble); Maria
in *Twelfth Night*; Ophelia in *Rosencrantz
And Guildenstern Are Dead*; Miss
Zampa in *La Grande Magia,
What The Butler Saw*, (Royal National
Theatre); Panthea in *A King and No
King*; Princess Natalie in *The Prince
of Homburg* (RNT Studio); *Playboy
of the Western World* (Farnham);
*The Pastoral Symphony; My Sweet
Rose; Othello; The Tempest* (Custard
Factory Theatre Company).

TV: *People Like Us; My Hero; Rhona*.

Radio: *Remplisson*.

Biographies

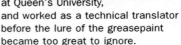

John O'Mahony
Fergal

Trained: Webber
Douglas Academy

Theatre: Includes
seasons of repertory at Worcester,
Chester, Cheltenham and Derby, where
he was voted 'Actor of the Year' and won
the 'Best Actor' award for his Puck in *A
Midsummer Night's Dream*. Also *Destiny*
(Half Moon); *Tales Of A City* (Croydon
Warehouse); *Boots For The Footless*
(Tricycle); Buddy (National Tour);
Germinal (Paines Plough); and *Mother
Courage* (Manchester Contact, director
Anthony Clark). Most recently he
appeared as Captain Ahab in *Moby Dick*
(The Gasteig Theatre, Munich; The Inter-
national Music-Theatre Festival, Volvos,
Greece; and on tour throughout Europe).

TV: *The Chief* (Anglia Films); *Brumbie*
(Channel 4) *Father Ted Christmas
Special* (Channel 4) and *By The Sword
Divided* (BBC).

Radio includes: For BBC Radio 4,
The Bagel Philosopher, *The Absentee*,
Anzacs Over England and *Child Of The
Forest*.

In 1996 John established *The Hungry
Grass*, a touring theatre ensemble
dedicated to epic theatre forms. His
first production *Pork Bellies* - hailed as
'the best show on the small scale for a
number of years' (Brighton Theatre
Festival), toured twice in the UK before
travelling to Ireland where it is presently
under development as a feature film,
(new title *3 Little Pigs* Besom
Productions in association with the Irish
Film Board). His latest play *Mushroom
Man* will be touring nationally in 2001.

Eileen Pollock
Maura

Eileen is Belfast
born and bred,
studied languages
at Queen's University,
and worked as a technical translator
before the lure of the greasepaint
became too great to ignore.

Theatre ranges from Oscar Wilde's
mother in Field Day's *St Oscar* to
Goldilock's mum in panto, from
the journalist in the original English
production of *Accidental Death Of
An Anarchist*, to Anna in Marie
Jones's *Women On The Verge* Of
HRT (Tour/West End), and from
Lady Macbeth to both Masha
and Olga in *The Three Sisters*
(but not at the same time).

TV: Lilo Lil' in the BBC sitcom *Bread*,
several TV plays and films including
Dear Sarah (RTE/Channel 4) and
Force Of Duty (BBC), and appearances
in *Civvies*, *Taggart* and *The Bill*.

Radio includes: Title roles in the 4
part series *The Pamela Mayers Show*,
and Monday play *Boudicca*.

Film: The brothel keeper Molly Kay
in Ron Howard's *Far and Away*, the
Scottish missonary Helen Pottinger
in Sydney McCarthy's *A Love Divided*,
the moneylender Mrs Finnucane in
Alan Parker's *Angela's Ashes* and
most recently, the magistrate in
Declan Lowney's newly released
Wild About Harry.

THE REP

Eileen has been invited to tour the United States in the spring with two one-woman shows, *Fight Like Tigers*, the story of Irish-American mineworkers' leader Mother Jones, and *Kathleen, Mother Of All The Behans*. She is also involved in W3KTC, an ongoing painting and storytelling project with painter James Foot.

Writer
Kaite O'Reilly

Winner of 1998 Peggy Ramsay Award for *Yard* at The Bush Theatre, London. Translated as *Slachthaus*, it ran for over a year at the Maxim Gorki Theatre, Berlin. Kaite has just written and directed her first short film for Channel 4/British Screen: *Mouth Screen Gems*, and her first full length film is currently in development with an Irish production company.

Lives Out of Step - experimental radio drama to be broadcast on BBC Radio 3 in early 2001.

Kaite is currently completing her first novel and working on commissions from Contact Theatre, Graeae Theatre and Sgript Cymru.

Director
Anthony Clark

Since joining Birmingham Repertory Theatre Company in 1990 as an Associate Director, Anthony has directed *The Seagull*, *Of Mice and Men*, *Macbeth*, *Saturday Sunday Monday*, *Cider With Rosie* (national tour), *The Threepenny Opera*,

The Pied Piper, *My Mother Said I Never Should*, *The Grapes of Wrath*, *The Atheist's Tragedy*, (1994 TMA/Martini Award for Best Director), *The Playboy of the Western World*, *Peter Pan*, *Pygmalion*, *The Red Balloon* (1995 TMA /Martini Award for Best Show for Children and Young People), *The Entertainer*, *Gentlemen Prefer Blondes*, *Pinocchio*, *Julius Caesar, Saint Joan* and new plays: *True Brit*, *Rough*, *Playing By the Rules* (Mentorn First Night Production Award), *Nervous Women*, *Syme* (a co-production with the Royal National Theatre Studio), and *Home Truths* by David Lodge. He has also directed *Confidence*, *Down Red Lane*, *Paddy Irishman, Paddy Englishman, Paddy...?, All That Trouble That We Had*, *Silence, My Best Friend* (which also completed a successful run at Hampstead Theatre) and *The Slight Witch* in The Door.

Anthony graduated from Manchester University Drama Department (RSC Buzz Goodbody Award 1979), spent two years directing at the Orange Tree Theatre, London and a year working with Tara Arts before being appointed Artistic Director of Contact Theatre in Manchester in 1984. At Contact Theatre his wide range of productions included new plays: *Face Value, Two Wheel Tricycle, McAlpine's Fusiliers, Green and Homeland*, classics: *Mother Courage and Her Children, Blood Wedding, A Midsummer Night's Dream, The Duchess of Malfi, To Kill a Mockingbird* (European premiere - Manchester Evening News Best Production Award 1987) and *Oedipus Rex*.

Biographies

^{THE}**REP**

His freelance directing credits include: *Dr Faustus* (Young Vic), *To Kill A Mockingbird* (Greenwich Theatre), *The Snowman* (Leicester Haymarket), *The Red Balloon* (Bristol Old Vic), *The Day After Tomorrow*, *Mother Courage and her Children* and *The Red Balloon* for the Royal National Theatre, and *The Wood Demon* (West End).

As a writer he has had the following plays produced: *Hand it to Them*, *Wake* and a translation of Tolstoy's *The Power of Darkness* at the Orange Tree Theatre, *Tidemark* at the RSC Thoughtcrimes Festival, *A Matter of Life and Death* at the Royal National Theatre, *Green* and musical adaptations of *The Snowman*, *The Little Prince* and *The Red Balloon* at Contact Theatre in Manchester and *The Pied Piper* and *Pinocchio* at Birmingham Repertory Theatre.

Designer
Rachel Blues

Trained: Edinburgh College of Art and Bristol Old Vic Theatre School.

For Birmingham Repertory Theatre Company: *Silence* by Moira Buffini

Designs include: *Top Girls* (BAC), *The Dove* (Warehouse Theatre Croydon); *Bouncers* (Octagon Theatre Bolton/Belgrade Theatre Coventry); *Car* (Theatre Absolute, Coventry Belgrade - winner of Fringe First), *Inmate Death* (Gate London). For the Coliseum Theatre, Oldham, *Rebecca*, *Brimstone and Treacle*, *Keeping Tom Nice*, *Lucky Sods*, *Second From Last in the Sack Race*, *Dead Funny*,

The Cemetery Club, *Dancin' in the Street* and costumes for *Alfie - The Musical*. For the Swan Theatre Worcester, *Charley's Aunt*, *Private Lives* and *Elsie and Norm's Macbeth*. In preparation: *Ham* (New Vic Theatre, Stoke).

Lighting Designer
Symon Harner

For Birmingham Repertory Theatre: The World Premieres of *The Tenant of Wildfell Hall*, *East Lynnen* and *The Slight Witch*; *A Shaft of Sunlight* (For Tamasha Theatre Company); *Playing by the Rules* (also at the Drill Hall, London); *Turn of the Screw*; National tours of *Metamorphosis* and *Kafka's Dick* (the latter being in collaboration with Lennie Tucker); *The Trial* (for The Mouse People) and *The Canal Ghost*. For The Door: *Perpetua; Trips;* The Transmissions Festival; *Silence* at Plymouth Theatre Royal and *My Best Friend* at The Rep (both re-lights of designs by Tim Mitchell). *My Dad's Cornershop.*

For the Birmingham Rep Youth Workshop: *Pinocchio*; *The Threepenny Opera*; Tony Harrison's *"V";* and *The Magic Toyshop* (also at the Edinburgh Festival in collaboration with Philip Swoffer). *Tales fom the Vienna Woods* and *The Hired Man* (Plymouth Theatre Royal). National Tour of Inamorata's *Pigtales* which opened at the (Bristol New Vic).

The Door is Birmingham Rep's theatre for new work. Our aim is to present an accessible, entertaining and challenging season of new plays each year; a season that provides a space for a range of contemporary voices; that reflects a diversity of style, subject matter and perspective, and creates a different experience of the theatre every time.

So, by the end of last season, we had taken you from a roof-top to a corner-shop; from Judea to Jamaica; from Moira Buffini's millennial medieval comedy, *Silence*; to the contemporary curry kitchens of Brum in *Balti Kings*; from one night in an African cave in Charles Mulekwa's drama, *A Time Of Fire* to another of acid childhood recriminations in Tamsin Oglesby's black comedy *My Best Friend*.

What's more, our shows are now consistently breaking their box office targets, bringing together younger and older audiences, first time and regular attenders and building an audience for new work made in Birmingham.

New plays for our programme come from a variety of sources. One is the writers' attachment scheme, which this year has been sponsored by Channel 4 Television. This provides an opportunity for writers to explore new ideas and to experiment. Both *Terracotta* by Jess Walters and Ray Grewal's *My Dad's Corner Shop* started life on the scheme as the briefest of outlines and went on to become successful productions last season.

We are now planning the new season for 2001 and with your support this new theatre for new work can only go from strength to strength.

Anthony Clark
Associate Artistic Director

Naomi Radcliffe in *The Slight Witch*

Transmissions

Transmissions is The Rep's training project aimed at nurturing the playwrights of the future. It gives twenty-five young people from across the region aged 12-25 the chance to develop their writing skills in a constructive and creative way.

The writers work closely with playwrights Noel Grieg and Carl Miller developing initial ideas into complete scripts through a series of workshops and constructive feedback. The scheme also allows participants to meet other young writers in a fun and inter-active environment, gives them the support and encouragement needed to extend their interest into a creative process and finally to see their work performed on stage at The Rep by professional actors in the Transmissions Festival in July 2001

For more information about Transmission contact Caroline Jester in the **Literary Department** at The Rep on **0121 245 2037.**

From Page to Stage

Designed to be an holistic experience of the process of writing and producing a new play, a place in the Page to Stage scheme includes:

• Hugely subsidised tickets for the plays in The Door, the equivalent of £3.00 per show.

• Scripts of the plays at cost.

• Workshops: two supporting workshops, the first in school to introduce the plays, and the second at the theatre with the writer and director.

• Afterdarks: discussion with the cast after the show

This package is available for FE, HE and sixth form students as well as Youth and Community groups (16+).

For further information about
Page to Stage please contact
the **Education Department on 0121 245 2093**.

Young Rep
The Rep's Youth Theatre

^{THE}REP

The Young Rep, a company for young people aged between 7 – 19, currently has 100 members who are committed to learning about drama and performance.

In the past year they have developed a range of performance and production skills with our in-house team, and participated in weekly workshops led by professional drama practitioners and directors.

In July the Young Rep presented their collaboration with playwright Michael Punter, an irreverent reworking of Aristophanes' classic satire *The Birds*, which received great reviews.

The Young Rep are currently working towards performances which will take place in The Door at the end of January. Each group is working with different styles of performance. The junior group are working on a visual interpretation of the Hans Christian Anderson classic, *The Little Tin Soldier*, the intermediates are producing *Do we never see Grace?*, a piece created by Noel Greig, a writer from the Transmissions project, while the seniors are working on a devised piece, based partly on *The Pedestrian* written by Ray Bradbury. All should provide fascinating and compulsive viewing.

The Young Rep welcomes young people from across the area. If you would like more information either about joining the Young Rep or forthcoming Young Rep productions, please contact the **Education Department on 0121 245 2093**.

The Birds

Kaite O'Reilly
Belonging

ff

faber and faber

First published in 2000
by Faber and Faber Limited
3 Queen Square, London WC1N 3AU
Published in the United States by Faber and Faber Inc.
an affiliate of Farrar, Straus and Giroux LLC, New York

Typeset by Country Setting, Kingsdown, Kent CT14 8ES
Printed in England by Intype London Ltd

A CIP record for this book
is available from the British Library

ISBN 0–571–20902–5

2 4 6 8 10 9 7 5 3 1

*This play is dedicated
to my family*

*and the Gilligans, Garveys,
Denneheys, Brennans . . .*

with thanks, gratitude and love

Characters

Maura
First-generation Irish immigrant. Married to Fergal.

Fergal
First-generation Irish immigrant. Older than Maura.
He is disengaged, yet open. Dying.

Aine
Second-generation immigrant. Birmingham-Irish.
Daughter to Maura and Fergal. Ferociously Irish.

Seaneen
As Aine, his older sister, except he identifies
himself as European.

Billy
First-generation Irish immigrant. From the North,
but he evades the issue. Friend of the Rourkes
and former fellow navvy/drinking partner to Fergal.

Speaker
(*also* Voice on Radio, Woman on Tape)
A mature woman, certainly of great presence,
if not age. See note on page 7.

Notes

Accents

It is essential that the Speaker and first-generation
Irish immigrants speak with strong, authentic
Irish accents (the Rourkes, North Dublin; Billy, Belfast
or elsewhere in the North). Aine speaks with a 'general'
watered-down Irish accent – partly self-fabricated.
Seaneen speaks with a soft Brummie accent,
but can 'do' a superb Irish accent.

Speaker

The role of Speaker is non-naturalistic.
She is *Seannachie* – Irish Gaelic for storyteller – but
a teller of tales also listens. She speaks. She actively
observes. She *witnesses*. She is not a ghost, a banshee,
nor the personification of Caithleen ni Houlihan,
old Mother Ireland herself. Speaker is not a
supernatural presence and it would be a
misinterpretation to present her as such.

*The action takes place in the Rourke family home,
Birmingham, on 16 March – the eve of St Patrick's Day;
then the morning of St Patrick's Day itself.*

The time is the present.

One

Speaker sits at a high vantage point overseeing the action. Below is a large comfortable kitchen. There are two exits – one stage right into the garden, one stage left into the house – and a door upstage leading to a toilet.

Speaker begins the following continuous monologue. There is a change in focus once the domestic setting becomes lit and inhabited. For a short period, the monologue appears to be in stereo – live from the Speaker, but also coming from a radio on the table in the kitchen. At the point indicated in the text, there is an aural cross-fade until her words come solely out of the radio. The recorded monologue should still be clearly audible, but the sense is of background noise, as though it were a radio programme Fergal is absent-mindedly listening to as he potters about the kitchen. It should be clear to an audience that the speech refers to Fergal, but he is oblivious to that – except perhaps for one moment when he listens hard or reacts to the speech, showing resonance/interest.

For Maura, once she enters and sets about preparing the breakfast, the radio might as well be playing a ballad she could hum along to. She does not acknowledge the speech in any way. Her sole response is after Fergal exits and she slows her efficient busy-ness. It is then, in her stillness, that the closing lines appear to voice what is in her own head.

Darkness.

Lights up on Speaker.

Speaker When he first come over in the 'sixties, he had been Fergal, son of the sons of the Rourke clan, his name copperplated in the Gaelic on his official papers. Accepted as a navvy in construction work, the assimilation began. Fergal became Fergie became Freddie. By the time he rose in the ranks to be a factory foreman, his official name on the payslip was Frederick O'Rourke, known to the lads as Paddy.

Paddy, when still Fergal, son of the sons of Rourke, did not consult his family nor sweetheart, the tender slow-smiling Maura, daughter of the parish, when considering emigration. What they said was of no consequence. He sought instead the knowledge of clay-handed labourers in each of the nine bars surrounding his birthplace; men who carried the eternity of soil in their fingerprints, the indelible whorl of clay worn hard into the skin. Emigration? Didn't they know about it all? Daughters and sons and brothers and sisters they had, flying off in silver planes headed for the future. Fathers and uncles and grandparents there had been, locked snug in their cabins, hopeful for the New World. Great-grandparents and ancestors there once were, hacking dry coughs over drum-tight swollen bellies, nailed forever in their floating caskets, destined for a land more fiendish than their own broken land.

Lights up slowly on domestic scene. Fergal stands stage left in the doorway, looking in. He wears a jumper and trousers pulled on over pyjamas.

Emigration? Oh yes, they knew all there was to edify on the subject. England was the place and the spot within it, Birmingham. Didn't they have a cousin going great guns in that part?

Fergal looks slowly and closely at objects in the room. It is like a homecoming, but without sentimentality. He begins making tea. It is clear from the quiet, careful way of handling himself that he is recuperating from a serious illness, such as a stroke.

Get a boat over and ask for him on the High Street.
Everyone'd know Paddy Murphy. He'd see you right.
Give you a place to lay your head and teach you the
ropes. The Irish looked after its own. He'd not mind
one iota. Would *cead mile failte* you all over the shop.
Well, didn't he have someone to go to, himself, in the
beginning? An address? Ah, now you have me, only hear
from him at Christmas, but go into any of the pubs and
ask. Everyone'd know him.

Everyone knew who Paddy was.

There was a century of Paddys.

*Fergal passes the radio and the speech is heard in
stereo.*

Speaker/Radio Paddy Murphy, Paddy Driscoll, Paddy
O'Shea, Paddy Bradley, Paddy Mahon, Paddy Finnegan,
Paddy Reilly, Paddy Gilligan, Paddy Keogh, Paddy
Flynn, Paddy This, Paddy That, Paddy Shite, Paddy
Thick, Paddy Bog, Paddy Paddy, Paddy Paddy –

*Without interrupting the rhythm, it cross-fades until it
is just the radio.*

Radio Paddy Rourke stood in what seemed a metropolis.
He asked a passer-by directions to Birmingham, blushing
red to his ears when the stranger laughed, saying he was
in it. No, Birmingham – Paddy Rourke insisted – the
High Street in Birmingham. He was looking for Paddy
Murphy. 'Aren't we all?' the stranger asked, before
walking away.

*Maura appears at the door stage left. Pained, she
watches Fergal slowly setting the table. He is oblivious
to her presence.*

A shrunken man, standing with suitcase, smiling wanly,
waiting for the brass band to appear. An angry man,
ashamed of his innocence, knuckles gripped white about

the wicker handle, whistling distractedly between gnashing, grinding, creaking, clenching teeth.

A commonplace man, the five punt note safety-pinned to his vest, weighted by the emblem of the Blessed Virgin, a present from Knock.

Maura snaps efficiently into preparing a fry-up – mushrooms, rashers, eggs, black pudding. She nods a greeting to him, no-nonsense. Silently they continue with their preparations – one slow, careful, almost not of this world; the other with a fluid grace, purpose.

A drunken man, toasting the health of Mythical Murphy, man of fiction, creation of twisted dreams gone sour, vomiting in the gutter, falling asleep in the first doorway, but never, ever, ever telling the truth in the fortnightly letters back home.

The story is taken up again by the Speaker, who delivers it live. Neither Fergal nor Maura hear or acknowledge Speaker.

Speaker So eloquently did the former Fergal write of his new-found prosperity, so carelessly did he enclose the foreign notes into the envelopes, his family believed the Murphy creation myth and pushed hard on his nuptials. For wasn't the time ripe for a joining of the clans? Fergal was going handsomely, his bi-monthly missives proved that. Maura was wistful for children and had taken to dancing with men from other parishes. A wedding should be now, at the opportune moment, when there still was time to fill the cradles, to over-spill with grand-children the English great house which they all knew was coming, as sure as the angels, into Fergal's grasp.

Fergal brings Maura a cup of tea, they almost circle one another as he passes her, taking his own cup upstage to the toilet. She watches him.

So they danced at their wedding feast in the summer, shy Maura pliant against his blistered hand in the small of her back. And she laughed as he poured the drinks down the guests' open throats, pouring away more money than he had earned in a year on one night's extravagance. An extravagance merely to be spewed into gutters on the stagger home.

He exits into the toilet. Maura takes the pan off the heat, postponing the cooking of breakfast mid-chore.

'O'Rourke's wedding! What a breakfast that was!' they would say in later years as Maura, stranded in the lodgings in England, watched the cockroaches crawl around the light socket, acquiescing in the lies by her silence.

She stands, reflecting.

Hollow-eyed Maura, dreaming of the fields at home, twisting the band round and round her finger. Round and round. Forever and ever. Life without end. She was pregnant.

Brusquely she switches off the radio moves her cup to the table, goes to sit, can't settle, takes out new, shop-bought clothes from a tapestry sewing bag. She sits at the table with her sewing, then rises abruptly, goes to the door stage left and roars up the stairs.

Maura Seaneen!

Satisfied, nodding to herself, she resumes her seat at the table and begins altering the clothes which do not fit correctly. Some time passes. Billy appears at the window, looks in, disappears. We hear him singing before he enters stage right. Maura doesn't so much as raise her eyes.

Billy
> And Ireland, isn't it grand you look
> Like a bride in her rich adorning.
> And out of my very heart of hearts
> I bid you the top of the morning.

He flourishes his hat, stands expectantly but ignored. A beat.

Maura That'll cut no ice with me.

He tries again ingratiatingly.

Billy Is your daddy in, sweetheart?

Maura Nor flattery, neither.

Billy Is it the woman of the house I'm addressing?

Maura continues sewing.

Woman of the house – for I imagine that is whom I do be addressing – woman of the house, might I inquire of your (*husband*) –

Maura Can't you come in the front way like any normal, decent person would, with a knock on the door and wiping your feet before entering?

Billy –?

Maura But no, it's round the back with not so much as a 'by your leave', wandering in like you were the King of the Tinkers, owning the place. Did they not teach you manners where you're from? (*She looks at him for the first time.*) Indeed they did not, I can tell by the cut of you. Nor style, neither.

Billy self-consciously fiddles with his hat, then his balding head.

Billy That's the head-work. Grass doesn't grow on a busy road.

Maura Nor in the desert, neither.

Billy goes to sit down.

Did I say you could sit?

Billy stands abruptly. Maura pours one cup of tea, for herself, from the pot on the table. Billy stands. An awkward pause. Billy takes a box of cook's matches from his pocket and puts it on the side. He waits to see any reaction from Maura, then takes out another, then another from other pockets. As he does so, he shakes each new box at her, then puts it on the side. She finally looks at him.

Billy They're for himself. I presume he still has the habit –?

Maura nods towards an uncompleted matchstick model of a farmhouse.

Is he around? It's just I need to see him and I'm in a bit of a hurry, y'know?

Maura Oh, I know. Enough of a hurry not to be in touch for six months.
There's been changes.

Billy What changes could come between two old pioneers like us, Maura? What could possibly affect – (*He begins to sit.*)

Maura Did I offer you a seat?

Billy (*standing abruptly*) Ah, now – there's no need –

Maura There's every need. We were desperate to get in touch; didn't know what'd happened to you; thought the earth'd lep' up and swallowed you.

Billy Jesus, Maura, I never knew you cared.

Maura I don't. You could go to hell in a chip pan for all I care, but Fergal . . . Where have you been? No answer at the house, the phone disconnected . . .

Billy I've been away – a big job on in Coventry. And I've gone mobile. I'm now a walky-talky. What use is a phone in a house to me? I'm on site twenty-four hours of the fucking day – excusing the language.

Maura Trouble?

Billy That word is not in my vocabulary.

Maura makes a disbelieving sound.

I'm a professional, thirty years in the trade –

Maura Well that's not stopping other builders from going under. The papers are full of it –

Billy I can see I've been away too long, you've forgotten who you're talking to.

Unimpressed, Maura takes a drop of tea from her china cup, continues sewing. Billy goes into a number.

It's Mr Bricks and Mortar you're looking at here! *Sa casa* is *ma casa* – your house is my house. No matter what I'm handling – construction work, renovation, managing a property –

Maura (*interrupting*) Like my own –

Billy (*interrupting*) Just like your own in Ireland. Whatever it is I'm doing – building a conservatory – sub-letting – whatever it is, in my hands that house is – well . . . it's safe as houses, isn't it? Might that be a pot of tea you have there brewing?

Maura It might. (*She drinks leisurely.*)

Billy And might it be Irish tea? Bewleys? Lyon's Green Label?

Maura Barry's best, sent over special from home.

Billy By the crateloads, what?

Maura We do get through a good lot in this house.

Billy I can well imagine: the kettle always on the hob, the pot going round, cups for everybody . . .

She drinks in silence, resumes sewing.

You'd be hard pressed to find a better brew in England, I bet. Though some say it's the water, not the same as home. Can't get a decent taste from an English tap. It's all the recycling. Been through you ten times already – or some other bugger – no wonder you do have to boil it. Is there one going spare? A cup going wanting?

Maura There might.

Billy For it's terrible thing, waste.

He watches her preparing another cup and putting Kimberly biscuits on a plate.

So . . . how's your better half?

Maura You'll see for yourself soon enough. (*Calls.*) Seaneen!

Billy I don't know why I ask. It'll take a silver bullet to make Fergal Rourke lie down.

Maura (*calls*) Seaneen! I'm hoarse with calling you!

She takes up the fresh cup and saucer, Billy prepares to receive it when Seaneen enters, expertly picking up the proffered cup, drinking it quickly on the move. Billy's empty hand falls to his side. Maura despairs of Seaneen's T-shirt, with a union jack shaped as a target emblazoned on the front.

And you're not going out in that.

Still on the move, Seaneen takes a handful of Kimberleys, stuffing them in his face. Maura snatches the plate back off him, guarding the 'visitor's biscuits'.

Maura And I don't trail the other side of Birmingham to get the Kimberleys for you to be ramming them down your gullet, not even touching the sides.

Seaneen No, you'd put them in a glass case – Exhibit A – look, but don't touch. (*Seaneen physically acknowledges Billy – but continues on a roll with his mother.*)

Maura Did you ever hear such a thing – a young fellamelad bla'guarding his mother?

Billy I did not.

Maura And lying in bed all day, wasting that lovely sunlight.

Seaneen It's ten o'clock in the morning!

Maura Exactly. When I was your age I would've been up for hours, helping with the milking . . .

Seaneen . . . And ploughing ten fields single-handed, I know.

Maura You don't know you're born.

Seaneen But it's Saturday. As in weekend. As in having a lie-in . . .

Maura The weekend was designed as a rest for those who've been working all week, not lazing in bed like some I could . . .

Seaneen So, Uncle Bill . . . long time no see . . .

Billy So I keep being told and less of the uncle. I'm a friend – that's a privilege – relatives are a given – you can't choose family – but friends . . .?

Seaneen manages to swipe another few biscuits off the plate.

Maura And let up with the Kimberleys! Whoever heard of anyone breakfasting on biscuits? What you need is a good fry. Sit down now, I'll get the pan on.

Seaneen I'm not hungry.

Maura It's being up half the night, drinking, does that.

Seaneen (*to Billy*) If you're after Dad, he's probably in the jacksie.

Maura And I don't care what you say, you're not going out in that rigmarole. You're a moving target.

Seaneen (*to Maura*) That's the idea.

Maura But a moving target for what, I don't know.

Seaneen (*to Billy, indicating a door nearby*) Give the door a knock.

Maura I hope you're not expecting to wear that tomorrow. You can't go on the Irish Day parade looking like a Rule Britannica.

Seaneen (*to Maura*) I'm not going. (*to Billy*) Used to be the cloakroom until we realised none of us had cloaks.

Maura Not going!

Billy hovers at a loss by the toilet door.

Seaneen Give it a good rap. He hides in there to get away from Jaws, here.

Maura But it'd be our first parade!

Seaneen (*to Maura, exiting*) So what I've never known, I've never missed.

Billy (*knocking door*) Fergal? Is that you in there?

Maura Come back here this minute. (*She follows Seaneen off.*) Seaneen!

> *The toilet flushes, Billy stands back, uncertain, agitated. He looks impatiently at the WC door, fidgets, wills Fergal to come out so they can speak privately, whilst they are temporarily alone. A beat. The door opens and Fergal comes out. It is clear his quiet, careful way of handling himself is new to Billy, who tries not to show his shock.*

Fergal I never thought then it could kill you.

> *He sits, as does Billy. A beat.*

I could lay my head down and die with the pain.

Billy Ah, now.

Fergal They never tell you that.

Billy Indeed, they do not.

Fergal Not a word about homesickness. Wouldn't have us off their hands otherwise. The little birdies flying from the trees.

Billy The nest.

Fergal Ah, you make another one somewhere else. A couple of sticks and you string your life through it.

Billy Precarious.

Fergal When the wind blows. And it does that well enough. Blows. And I do get to thinking we can walk on the air, for what else is it sustains us?

Billy Graft.

Fergal Ah! We do that all right. The skin peeling from the hands. The feet walking on air. We must be miraculous creatures.

Billy Dazzling.

Fergal Dazzling and dazed.

Billy The Irishman's natural condition. And none knows better than ourselves. Isn't that right? Ha, Fergal?

Fergal Ah, indeed.

Billy So. (*Beat.*)
   I wanted a word with ye. (*Beat.*) I wanted to speak plain on what could be a difficult subject. I want you to know I'm not ungrateful. I'm not the type to bite off the hand that fed me. I remember my dues and recall who thought well of me when I started out. I'm grateful for the money you gave me, the backing. But a sleeping partner shouldn't sleep too deep, and it's even more important when you're friends. D'you know what I'm saying, Fergal? Are ye with me on this? I'm disappointed now, for I wanted to come here today with a bouquet of notes for you – as thanks. I had a bit of money there, a little bit put away for you and Maura, tidy sum, from the, y'know – (*He checks they are alone.*) – from the investment in the business. But. And there lies a tale. You see what I'm getting at? For sometimes the intention exists, but not the means, d'you get me? And I'm distraught, balling up me courage here in me hands, for it's a hard thing to say and admit and to tell, but –

Fergal (*interrupting*) Should I know you?

Billy Know me?

   Billy is surprised at the question. Maura enters.

Should ye know me?

   Maura looks at Billy nervously. He takes his cue from her expression.

No, not at all. It's been a while . . .

21

Fergal I should, shouldn't I?

Maura Fergal, it's –

Fergal Sssh, don't tell me.

Maura recommences cooking the fry-up for Fergal throughout the next section.

It's on the tip of my . . . Fagan. Fagan the Milk, isn't that right?

Billy Jimmy Fagan, milkman –

Fergal There now!

Billy – used to do the rounds along Sparkbrook.

Fergal What did I tell you?

Billy He's dead. I'm William McFarland. The construction gaffer . . . Used to be a navvy, met you when working the roads . . . It's Billy! Billy the Muck. Worked the stables in Knowle – used to cart round the manure to the posh wans for their rose beds at the weekend.

Fergal Billy.

Billy McFarland. The Muck.

Fergal Ah . . .

Billy Now d'you have me? Used to be sweet on Trisha Brennan, barmaid at the Antelope . . .? She wouldn't have me on account of –

Maura – the smell?

Billy The difference in faith, what with me being Jewish.

Maura snorts derisively.

I'll have you know I come from a long line of distinguished Irish Jewmen.

Maura You're an Orangeman if ever I saw one.

Billy I am not. Wasn't my grandmother's side Russian – came over to Dublin at the turn of the century to escape the Bolshies. I'm a White Russian –

Maura So they called you William, after Tolstoy?

Billy After the other side of the family, French. Story goes they were carting over guns and fighting talk from Madam Guillotine, to help our own small revolution in 1798. They ran ashore and were hidden by the locals – ended up doing what most of the other foreigners did – settled down, married a local girl and became more Irish than the Irish. What are we but a mixed breed fleeing one riot or another?

Maura God bless neutral Ireland with her talent for parody, gobshite and fence-sitting.

Fergal Have you noticed they're not so keen to smile here as we would, at home?

Maura and Billy fall silent.

That blank spot in the eye. Dead.

Billy But not dazzled.

Fergal Definitely not dazzled. Mute. Suspicious. Frightened maybe but not impressed. The dazzle never enters them. The barricades are up against impression.

Billy Ah, it's a shame.

Maura Shame indeed they would put on us.

Fergal If the sky is murky and the rain falls down, that's our fault. Brought it in with us, the filthy weather, when we clambered over the mud flats.

Billy Mud-crawlers.

Fergal I came over on the cattle boat. Could hear them lowing and moaning beneath my feet the whole journey. Wretched. Wretched I was with my mother at home and me standing on wood over water with the beasts below.

Billy Ah, now.

Fergal A hundred stories the same. And they'd never think of telling you.

Maura They would not.

Fergal For how would they shift us, otherwise? With dynamite, perhaps. That semtex. Gunpowder. Blow us all up to kingdom come – which is where we go, anyway, so we save them the bother.
   (*to Billy*) You do look now, you know, familiar.

Billy Knew each other, man and boy.

Fergal Did we?

Billy Oh, the skirmishes we had, great fun altogether.

Fergal Is that so?

Billy Drinking partners on a good few occasions. Terrible thirst. Never sated. Once, now, once – we were well tanked up, out drinking after hours in some dive. Next thing you looked at your watch and let such a cry out of you it was so late – said the missus'd take a bite out of you – begging your pardon Maura – so didn't you only decide to hitch a lift on the back of a lorry – one of these intercontinental jobs, drives through the night. So we jumped on the tailbar of this yoke and it only sped up, going like the blazes, hell for leather down the Stratford Road . . .

Fergal Were we destroyed?

Billy Not at all. It stopped at the traffic lights at the Mermaid and we lep' off, safe as safe.

Fergal Wasn't that great?

Billy And nobody knew a thing of it to this day but ourselves.

Fergal There, now.

Billy Not a soul knew, not even the driver.

Fergal nods once. The atmosphere is strained. A beat. Maura puts the fry on a plate, arranges it carefully, is about to place it down before Fergal when:.

Fergal I think I'll have a lie down now, Maura.

Maura But you've only just . . . As you like.

Fergal Be ready and rested for the big day, what?

Maura (*to Billy*) The St Patrick's Day Parade.

They nod their heads, standing awkwardly, Maura with the plate of fried food in her hands as, painfully slowly, Fergal rises and gathers his things together. Maura speaks as he organises himself.

The whole family's off on it tomorrow, please God, all being well.

Beat, more nodding heads.

All but passes the house – goes by there the end of the road there and we've never gone.

Billy Have you not?

Maura No. Would you credit that? Virtually past that window and not one of us have marched.

Head-nodding.

Though it wasn't on, of course, for a good few years.

Billy Of course.

Maura For a while there singing and dancing and making proud to be Irish wasn't –

Billy – appropriate.

Maura No.

Billy No.

Maura No. Still, you can't be making acts of contrition all your life . . .

Billy Indeed you can't.

Maura And we'd hear it go by, the last few years, sitting there in the chair, with the accordions and the flutes –

Fergal is slowly exiting.

– people singing and cheering and I thought this year, what with the peace talks and everything now behind us, please God, this year we'll go, all of us together . . .

Fergal has made it to the door. He salutes Billy.

Fergal Nice seeing you again. Good luck, now, Jimmy.

Maura Billy.

Fergal What?

Maura I'll give you a call before too long.

He exits. Pause.

I do it myself at times, get all confused and forgetting.

She looks at the plate in her hand, wavers, not sure what to do with it, then puts it down decisively in front of Billy.

There, now.

She nods him to sit and eat. He does, with appetite.

And if you do think he's bad now, you'd have wanted to see him when he come out of the hospital.

Billy No, no, he's grand.

Maura They didn't want to sign him out, but his heart was set on it, you know, for the big day.

Billy He'll be fine, Maura. Not a bother on him. It just – took me by surprise.

Maura He comes in and out of it. Sometimes he's more lucid than others –

Billy I had no idea.

Maura We were trying to get in touch with you –

Billy Right.

Maura – when he got bad, but also to discuss the arrangements.

Billy looks blank.

Moving back . . .? To my farm . . .? You know it's always been our intention.

Billy (*faintly*) Fergal never . . .

Maura . . . I'm grateful to you for looking after it for me – dealing with the rent and everything –

Billy But Maura, Fergal never . . .

Maura . . . I'm in charge now.
I want to go home, Billy. It's time I went home.

Billy To Ireland.

She nods.

You want your house back?

She nods.

Well then.

Billy's appetite is abating. He tries to eat with the same steady enthusiasm but plays with the food.

27

Billy Have you written to the tenants, giving them notice?

Maura No.

Billy Approached them in any way?

She shakes her head.

Phoned, or –

Maura I thought that was your job.

Billy It is. It just would've given them a little longer to find somewhere new, but not to worry. (*Something of the old confidence comes back.*) I'll sort it. I'm on the case. And I don't want you to give this one more second's thought, right? You've enough on your plate. (*He pushes the food from him.*)

Maura Thanks.

Billy Is Fergal looking forward to it?

Maura Well, he doesn't rightly . . . (*Her words die away.*)

Billy He won't find it strange?

Maura Strange – going home?

Billy I'm sure it helps being in a familiar place, amongst familiar things.

Maura You won't know him when we're back a week. A week back in Ireland and he'll be his old self.

Billy I meant here, Maura. Isn't it familiar here? You've had this place more than twenty –

Maura It's not the same.

Billy The kids were reared here. All the memories – the life that's gone on in these rooms . . .

Maura This is a house. It's not home. Not real home.

Billy Right.

Maura There's no comparison.

Billy Right.
And he's fit for the travelling?

Maura And why wouldn't he be?

Billy (*suddenly ashamed of himself*) No reason. No reason at all.

Maura Sometimes *I'm* forgetting things all the time myself. I do. Just the other day I was thinking of how pleased Mammy would be with us finally going home and the feast she'd make for us and a little box of groceries standing by with her pullets' eggs and butter, with our own milk fresh from the cow. And I was thinking what present I should bring back for her, and wondering which of her dresses she might be wearing when we arrive – maybe that blue one with the flowers I always admired – and how she'd look when I saw her and then I remembered she's been gone these past eleven years – stone dead and never coming back – but I'd forgotten it, even for one moment. It was just the same when I had the radio on the other day tuned to an Irish station and at twelve o'clock the bells came on and I couldn't for the life of me recall what they were for. I'd forgotten the angelus, just like I'd forgotten my mother was no longer with us any more and sometimes I have to hold on tight not just to myself, but to the edge of the table or the sideboard or some such, for leverage, to anchor, for otherwise I think I'd lose hold of myself.

Billy nods a thanks towards the unfinished breakfast and begins making the motion of leaving.

Billy Let's hope we'll have a fine day for it, tomorrow, so.

Maura Indeed. Weather forecast said there might be rain.

Billy And we don't want damp green ribbons do we, now? Hordes out on the streets looking like drowned rats.

Maura I hear they're dyeing the Guinness green this year.

Billy Some Yank invention. Probably just the head.

Maura We've been here long enough, Billy. It's time we were going home.

Billy When I left Ireland, I had a share in a farm with a couple of head of cattle and a Massey Ferguson rusting in the yard. (*He busies himself with leaving, not looking at her.*) Best bring an umbrella with you tomorrow. You don't want yourself or the big man to catch a chill.

Maura I'll do that.

About to exit, Billy pauses.

Billy Thirty years later and what have I now? A pocket full of change with the face of a woman on the front that'd frighten sheep. Maura, I'm – (*He controls himself.*) away to see a man about a dog.

Maura Making more of that money, ha?

Billy That's right. We tycoons have to do something to keep us occupied and out of trouble. I'll see myself out.

Maura Will you not stay for a cup of tea?

He raises his hand to her, bows out.

At least look in on us, again, later, when Fergal's up. He'd be glad of the company . . .

Billy has gone. Maura stands, a beat.

(*barely audible*) Home.

She sees the breakfast plate, removes it from the table, stands staring at her hands. A beat.

Speaker The immigrant's map. Borders. Boundaries. The lines in her palm – stone walls running across the land.

Maura goes to wash the breakfast things, stops, grips the sink hard, clings on, it passes. She breathes, looks out, in her memory begins walking home across the fields.

Maura Dennehy's . . . the widow Cross . . . Hanratty's field . . .

Speaker (*simultaneously*) Once, one farm, a large flank of land, halved and again quartered, given in choice cuts to keep the sons at home.

Maura My uncle's meadow . . . the Nulties . . . the Nulties . . . my father's land.

Speaker Divided, sub-divided, little left but an outcrop of rock. Tiny fields, hemmed in tight with man-made stitches. The sons left, anyway. A harvest of stones.

Maura has arrived home in her mind.

Maura Eleven o'clock. Put the bread on to soak for the turkeys, slops to cook for the sow. Empty the potato peelings out onto the compost. Fill the kettle with fresh water so it's clean boiling for Dado's cup of tea – he does taste the stale water that's been on the range all morning.

Speaker Her litany. Her actions of the hour.

Maura Polish the shoes – soles and uppers – so they won't see the wear when kneeling during Mass. Put yesterday's news under the oilcloth on the table. Check the salt cellar.

Maura's daughter Aine enters from the back door, smoothly taking over the litany.

Aine Wipe the neck of the sauce bottles before putting them on the table. See that there's enough margarine in the dish – butter's full of cholesterol, bad for Dad's arteries – fill the jug with *skimmed* milk –

Maura – and take no arguments from your father.

Aine swings recording equipment, various books and video cassettes onto the table, which Maura eyes disapprovingly.

Taping fools prattling on about their sad lives again, were we?

Aine Preserving oral traditions for the edification of future generations, yes.

Maura Some things are best left private, unsaid.

Maura moves the recording equipment aside and stands expecting further packages.
A beat. There are none.

You weren't successful?

Aine No.

Maura You didn't get any?

Aine Not a jot.

Maura None?

Aine shows empty hands.

Did you try everywhere?

Aine Yes.

Maura And not a –

Aine No.

A beat.

Maura Would it be too late if we tried tomorrow? Perhaps they're not getting it in until the morning?

Aine shrugs. A breath. The women look at each other, then away.

I knew we should have grown our own.

Aine It doesn't take.

Maura Have a little pot there on the window-sill.

Aine It mutates.

Maura Enough sprigs for ourselves, maybe a few for the neighbours.

Aine They're English.

Maura The prices the shops charge . . .

Aine What would they be doing with it when they're English?

Maura Could get a flight over to Shannon, pick your own and still have change.

Aine Lots of people get their families to send it over.

Maura Who?

Aine Uncles. Cousins.

Maura They're all in America.

Aine Wrapped in tin foil in the envelope, the roots in damp cotton wool.

Maura It'd be dead by the time it arrived.

Aine But at least it'd be authentic.

Maura Withered.

Aine But authentic.

Maura No good would come from it. Unlucky. Going round with dead shamrock on your chest.

Aine But it'd be the real thing.

Maura Tempting fate. You'd be as well picking some clover from the garden.

Aine That's cheating!

Maura Or some cress from the greengrocer's. No one would know the difference.

Aine Of course they would!

Maura Then tell them it was grown from seed and mutated. After all, you can't grow shamrock in English soil.

Aine Is that meant to be me?

They look at each other.

You're very funny, aren't you?

Maura Hilarious.

Aine We should put you on the stage.

Maura I'd make millions.

Aine I'll dig out the old tricolour pins.

Maura You do that.

Maura exits. Aine takes down an old rusting tin, stuffed with papers and oddments. She begins searching through it at the table, stops, goes to the fridge and opens it, looking inside for several seconds. She takes a can of soft drink out, settles back at the table, drinking and looking for the pins. Seaneen enters behind Aine, sees she is alone, checks the door for Maura, then puts his arm up the chimney of the open fire and pulls down a box of Irish cigarettes.

*Pleased, he cadges a fag, and lights up, cocky and full
of himself. He goes to replace the box but pauses,
takes another fag which he puts behind his ear. Aine
doesn't look at him when she speaks, merely continues
sorting through the tin, finding the flag-pins.*

Aine Well, isn't he the clever little maneen? Finally
worked out Mam's hiding-place. Are you enjoying that?
The unmistakable aroma of an Irish cigarette . . . (*She
sniffs deeply.*) Mmmm . . . turf burning. Taste different
from your usual brand?

Seaneen Suppose.

Aine I imagine it would seeing it's been smoked like a
good kipper up there for the past ten years.

Seaneen What?

Aine They probably date back to Nanny's funeral, put
out of temptation's way, to be used solely in emergencies.
She'll have your guts for garters, if she discovers half the
packet's gone.

Seaneen But I've only had –

Aine I'm afraid you'll have to pay the forfeit for being a
bit slow on the up-take.

Seaneen But you don't smoke.

Aine Now. I've had recourse to the odd one over the
past few years. And sorry to disappoint you, but there's
no brownie points for finding her hiding-place. It's pretty
obvious when you think about it.

He looks at her blankly.

Come on, Sean, stop being the wooden-top. The stories
she was reared on.

Speaker Civil war.

Aine Gunmen on the run . . .

Seaneen I always switched off.

Speaker Priest holes.

Aine False chimney breasts . . . It was the first place I looked.

Seaneen Congratulations.

Aine And I don't remember you not listening.

Seaneen You've a poor memory, then.

Aine You were as avid as I was. More so. Sitting wrapped in an eiderdown, eating sugar sandwiches, asking 'your Mammy' to tell you about 'the guns'.

Seaneen I was not.

Aine You were so.

Seaneen I wasn't.

Aine You were.

Seaneen You've got it wrong –

Aine I was there! I saw you! And I'm older than you, anyway.

Seaneen What's that supposed to mean?

Aine Whatever you like.

A beat, perhaps laughter.

Seaneen I remember that biscuit tin.

Aine looks at it, considers.

Aine Uncle Vernon.

Both And Aunty Mamie . . .

Seaneen mimicks his aunt, but with a superb Irish accent.

Seaneen 'Ah, g'wan, a little shortbread, it'll do you no harm, sure what's in it?'

Aine (*mimicking*) 'A dab of flour and water, that's all.'

Seaneen 'And you could do with a little something. Your stomach walls are merging; your belly thinks your throat's been cut. Go on, go on, you will . . . '

Aine Her orange lipstick! Was always here, on the front of her teeth.

Seaneen And his Bobby Charlton hairstyle.

Aine A few strands slicked over with Brylcream.

Seaneen I used to pray it wouldn't be windy. A breeze'd hinge up his hair, like cutting the top off a boiled egg. It gave me nightmares.

Aine And I hated kissing her. It was always wet and whiskery. She had a little moustache on her top lip.

Seaneen . . . Which is more than he had, poor bugger.

Aine And they'd bribe us to sing, with the butterscotch and liquorice toffees.

They all sing, slightly overlapping, Aine finishing last.

Speaker (*sings*)
  'Oh Danny Boy, the pipes, the pipes, are . . . '

Seaneen (*sings simultaneously*)
  'If you're Irish, come into the parlour . . . '

Aine (*sings*)
  'Oh we're off to Dublin in the green, in the green,
  Where the bayonets glisten in the sun . . . '.

Seaneen You all right, then?

Aine Yeah. How 'bout you?

Seaneen Can't complain. I'd like to, but I'm not allowed.

Aine Is it terrible?

Seaneen Happy families major-time. And the priest is always here, or some biddy from the Legion of Mary. Praying. Or singing. One had a melodeon with her the other day. It was 'Cling to the Rugged Cross' and 'Jesus Wants Me for a Sunbeam' dawn to dusk.

Aine You're joking.

Seaneen A slight exaggeration.

Aine But Mam was never . . .

Seaneen She's desperate. Try anything. Even considered a laying-on-of-hands by some nutter who speaks in tongues until I convinced her it was the devil's work. Frightened her with the prospect of Dad being possessed.

Aine But doesn't he . . .

Seaneen . . . Away with the fairies. Cloud-cuckoo-land. Could take him to Lourdes and he'd still think he was in the front room.
Of some farmhouse.
Up the top of a boreen.
In darkest Eire.

Aine Medication?

Seaneen Fuck knows. One thing's for certain, there's times I wish I wasn't here.

Aine You don't have to be.

Seaneen Is that an invite then?

Aine What?

Seaneen To crash at yours?

Aine No.

Seaneen Come on . . .

Aine Find your own pit.

Seaneen Aine.

Aine You're a big boy, now. No need to be tied to the Mammy's apron strings, nor muscle in on your big sister, either.

Seaneen Love life active?

Aine None of your business.

Seaneen Then why . . . ?

Aine Get your own place. God sake, be independent for once.

Seaneen As in – I'm not now?

Aine You know what I mean.

Seaneen As in – can't even piss without somebody's help?

Aine I didn't say that.

Seaneen As in – I'm a crap useless piece of humanity who hasn't grown up yet?

Aine And this is why I never get involved with Irish men.

Seaneen Woah! A low-flier, over the head, you lost me on that one.

Aine (*simultaneously*) Absolutely ruined. No good to God nor woman.

Seaneen And anyway I was born here.

Aine Promise you the birds in the bushes, but you'll catch them yourself. And no, I don't want to talk about it.

    A beat.

Aine Can't you move in with friends?

Seaneen All students. No money.

Aine Ever heard of working?

Seaneen Don't start.

Aine Don't complain, then. You'd probably be over every morning anyway for your breakfast. And clean laundry.

Seaneen Just let myself in with my own key and be discovered sitting at the table sorting through the family papers.

Aine I'm helping Mam.

Seaneen Taking stuff from the fridge without asking, never mind if it belongs to somebody else . . .

Aine I was out trying to find shamrock for her, while you were still snoring.

Seaneen Wander in and out without responsibility . . .

Aine And now I'm finding the flag-pins.

Seaneen . . . then fuck off to peace and quiet and never mind about the rest of us.

Aine Aaah . . . poor Seaneen.

Seaneen Sean.

Aine Isn't life hard?

Seaneen Don't bother finding one of them for me.

Aine Sorry?

Seaneen Your nationalistic bloody flag-pins. I'm not going.

Aine What?

Seaneen And I've told Mom.

Aine But – what harm would it do you? It's not like we'll be carrying burning crosses, or terrorising the locals. It's the St Patrick's Day Parade, for chrissake. A bit of fun. A laugh. You don't have to do anything but be there!

Seaneen No thanks. Join some piddling little group of prats –

Aine (*overlapping*) It's the biggest gathering this side of New York.

Seaneen – who're old enough to know better poncing around dressed like leprechauns –

Aine That's not –

Seaneen – whilst their kids tie their legs in knots trying to be Michael Flat –
  Oh! Did you hear? They found the missing link.

Aine What?

Seaneen It was on the telly – this book. This really famous book –

Aine Yeah . . .?

Seaneen Been missing years – decades – centuries really –

Aine And . . .

Seaneen It was found. This book – 'Irish Dancing Volume Two: What To Do With The Upper Body' (*He mimes a drum roll and cymbals clash.*) I'm not going. I'd rather be stabbed.

Aine Seaneen . . .

Seaneen Sean. And I can't see why the oldies can't do what they usually do: have a pint at the local or – d'you remember when we were kids? Them dances at St Anne's.

Aine Like being part of an underground sect – smuggled in under cover so the locals didn't know what we were celebrating, like it was something to be ashamed of.

Seaneen The bar: (*Irish accent*) 'Will you have a mineral?' and me thinking it must be a geology club. (*accent*) 'I'll have a quartz . . . or, go on, I'll be a divil – make that a bit of granite.'

Aine Seaneen . . .

Seaneen (*unstoppable, on a roll*) But that was nothing compared to Conlan's parties, d'you remember? The bath full of Brew XI – from those six pint tins . . .? And the mammies all tiddly on Babycham and Cherry B. (*laughing*) There was always some sad bastard in the front room playing the Wolfe Tones and singing 'A Nation Once Again' and Mom down trying to hush him up, frightened the neighbours'd hear and send Special Branch around to capture a cell of the IRA.

Aine It's not funny.

Seaneen I think it's fekkin' hilarious.

Aine You would.

Seaneen Got it in one, bab. And I have to say, I'm deeply impressed. There's me reminiscing and you didn't so much as twitch to put on your DAT. (*He goes for her recording equipment on the table.*) That takes some restraint. Have you had it surgically removed or are you going to meetings? (*mimicking her*) 'My name is Aine Rourke and I'm an oral history addict. I'm addicted to recording stories, reminiscence, any common or garden personal trivia . . . '

She retrieves her equipment from him.

Aine At least I've got a job.

Seaneen Oooh!

Aine And one that serves a purpose.

Seaneen You are much loved by the blue rin – the *emerald* rinse brigade. They're all lining up to tell you about their operations. (*accent*) 'I'm a martyr to the varicose veins' and how MI5 blocked their careers in local government because their dads used to run guns for Michael bloody Collins. Allegedly.

Aine That's closer to the truth than you think.

Seaneen I know it is. I've read some of your pamphlets – your (*right-on voice*) er – community publishing.

Aine Have you really?

Seaneen Yup. I just don't think you have to be so po-faced about it.

Aine But it wasn't fair. It was racist.

Seaneen That's life. Shit happens. Look on the bright side.

Aine Any more illuminating clichés?

Seaneen (*considers*) No.

Aine Have you finished?

Seaneen (*considers*) Yes.

Aine I still think you ought to come with us on the parade.

He looks bored.

It'll take half a day.

He is unresponsive.

Is that really too much to ask?

Seaneen They've never bothered to go before.

Aine This year's different.

Seaneen Oh yeah, how?

Aine 'Cause it's their last opportunity. Our last opportunity to go as a whole family.

He is still unmoved.

You're going to break their hearts.

Seaneen Oh, stop.

Aine This means so much to them, especially now, with Da . . .

Seaneen Don't . . . Mom's already given me GBH with the emotional cudgel.

Aine Then why . . .?

Seaneen I just haven't the interest.

Aine It's half a bloody day . . .

Seaneen I know!

Aine So why . . .?

Seaneen Just leave it!

Aine Please . . .

Seaneen No.

Aine Seaneen!

Seaneen And I wish you'd stop calling me that stupid fucking name . . .

Aine (*overlapping*) I'm sorry, I –

Seaneen . . . making me sound like some (*accent*) cute fucking hoor . . .

44

Aine (*overlapping*) We've always called you that since you were a little kid –

Seaneen . . . put a flashing sign over my head why don't you – bog trotter, spud eater . . .

Aine We can't change it, you've always been Seaneen . . .

Seaneen Like you've always been Aine?

She is pulled up short. A beat. Calmer. Colder.

Sorry, but I'm not interested.

Aine You used to be.

Seaneen Just . . . (*leave it*).

He begins to leave.

Aine So when did you lose 'the interest'?

Seaneen About the time you acquired 'the accent'.

Aine grabs the empty drinks can from the table and throws it, missing him as he ducks out of the door stage right. Maura witnesses this as she enters stage left.

Maura Aine!

Aine Well he . . . (*started it*).

Seaneen's head reappears round the back door. He mimics her voice and accent.

Seaneen (*simultaneously*) Mammy, Sean's bold, he . . .

Aine throws a box of matches at him, missing him again. He exits into the garden. Maura watches coolly, then gathers Fergal's matchstick model house and matches, bringing them to small table by the armchair.

Maura You'll have me crucified between you. I don't know who's the worst – the robber on me left or you on me right.

45

Aine So you're Jesus Christ, now.

Maura Did you not know? I'm like you. I can walk on water. (*She collects both tin and matches.*) And I'll have no more of this *craic* under my roof. When both of you are together it's like the terrible two's all over again. No – you're worse than a child.

Aine He asked for it.

Maura He did in his tail.

Aine He annoyed me.

Maura He can play you like a fiddle and what's more, you enjoy it.

Aine I do not.

Maura makes a disbelieving sound.

He won't come to the parade.

Maura He'll come.

Aine makes a disbelieving sound. They look at one another.

And you're only encouraging him, reacting like that. He takes the opposite position just to rile you and more fool you, you fall for it every time.

Aine So shoot me.

Maura I won't have that language in my house.

Aine So evict me.

Maura You think you're very clever.

Aine I don't.

Maura It's in his nature to be contrary. (*exiting*) Just as it's yours to be the expert and always in the right.

Aine is about to follow Maura, answering back at this perceived unfairness, when Fergal enters slowly. Aine smiles, mood changed. He vaguely acknowledges her and sits apart, by the farmhouse kit. He takes up a box of matches, lights one, blows it out, puts the stick safely by. After a pause, the action is repeated and continued throughout the scene. Aine watches. Maura, entering with a pillow, glances in Aine's direction warningly. Aine settles back at the table, ostensibly looking for the pins. Maura positions the pillow behind Fergal's back, then begins sifting flour, to make soda bread.

Maura He was only in there, asleep on the chair. The chair! And that lovely orthopaedic bed beside him! Unused! (*Beat.*) Bolt upright I'm telling you, dozing in the chair! (*Beat.*) Imagine!

Fergal I'm well able for it. I slept sitting up first month I was here.

Maura You did in your tail.

Fergal In a cinema seat.

Maura Don't be listening to him.

Fergal Fresh off the boat, looking for lodgings.

Maura Him and his inventions.

Fergal Couldn't find any. No one'd have me.

Speaker No blacks, dogs or Irish.

Fergal They never tell you that.

Speaker No tinkers, no coloureds.

Fergal Indeed they do not.

Speaker Handwritten in windows. Printed black in the paper.

Fergal No Irish need apply.

Maura Fergal Rourke, I think you're talking in your sleep. That's what comes from sleeping bolt upright. Gives you delusions.

Aine So where did you go?

Fergal The all-night showing at the Piccadilly Picture House in Sparkhill.

Speaker The cheapest doss-house, filled with Irish farm-boys dreaming of posses and ranches as cowboys cantered across the screen.

Fergal You'd tip the usher and she'd wake you in time for your shift –

Maura Did you ever hear such nonsense?

Fergal And then a kip, it was –

Maura Don't be showing me up.

Fergal – with a share in a bed –

Maura Fergal!

Fergal – occupied in eight hour shifts.

Maura Will you stop it?

Aine Mam.

Fergal A Scottish builder.

Maura I'm not having this!

Fergal A Jamaican working nights at the car factory.

Maura I'm warning you.

Aine Sssh.

Fergal Then me, a navvy. Three heads on one pillow, but not at the same time.

Maura That's it! I'm getting my coat!

She wipes her hands of pastry and stalks across, about to put her hand on her coat when Aine gets in front of her, blocking her path. This is obviously a threat from childhood, which still wields its power and the automatic response.

Aine (*very fast*) Don't go, Mam, we're sorry, we didn't mean it, didn't mean to upset you, did we, Da? We didn't, I promise. We won't do it again.

Maura takes her hand away from her coat, straightens her clothing and returns in silence to her baking. Several beats.

Maura We've always been decent in this family. (*Beat.*) No matter what's happened, we've always been that. (*Beat*) Clean, decent, honest. And that's how we got on.

Aine Yes, Mam.

Maura And I'm no good now for the baking. The anger's gone into the bread, poisoned it, it'll stick in the throat.

Aine Leave it to rest for a while.

Maura I don't want to hear another word of this, is that clear? And if I find anything's been carried out of this house and you know what I mean young lady . . . some nonsense mentioned to anyone else, whether you work with them or not . . . it'll be just as well your father and I are going home to Ireland, for I'd never be able to show my face around here again. Have I made myself understood?

Aine Yes.

Maura For you do have a strange idea of pride, girl, and I tell you for nothing, it's a million miles away from mine. I've washing on the line.

Maura exits into the garden. Aine looks at her father, away.

Aine Da?

Fergal continues his lighting and extinguishing of matches and doesn't respond.

Are you going back home. To Ireland. Da? I know Mam wants to. Do you?

Fergal Want. There's a word.

A beat. Aine has the idea of recording Fergal. Surreptitiously she switches on her DAT, aiming for an informal recording of 'father reminiscing as daughter makes the family soda bread'. However, it soon becomes clear she doesn't know how to bake. She perseveres as she feels she ought to have absorbed this knowledge. Her cack-handedness in the kitchen is almost comical, her speech slightly arch. She is earnest, but trying too hard.

Aine Don't you think it's strange how things turn out, Da? That whole generation of immigrants you were part of, coming over here, building the English cities, doing the jobs the locals wouldn't do, and now the shoe's on the other foot. Ireland's the economic miracle, now. The Celtic tiger purring away . . . There's not enough navvies in Ireland to deal with the property boom – can you imagine? A shortage of fellas with shovels! (*She looks to see if her words are having an effect. It is negligible. Then, more seriously*) The best export has always been the people and now they want us back.

A beat.

D'you want to go? Da? It's just if you do – could I . . .?

Fergal You have to remember in them days, once you went you never came back. Nobody ever saw your face again.

50

Speaker You were gone for good.

Fergal When I was going, I argued with my mother. She said 'I wish I was burying you instead of letting you go to England.' But I went, anyway.

Speaker It changed the landscape. A great tidal wave of people, quitting the place.

Aine grows concerned that the DAT is not actually switched on and tries to check without drawing Fergal's attention to her actions.

Fergal I wasn't the only one who left secretly or in anger. Disappearances were not uncommon. Plenty just upped and went. There was always someone from home that had a relative missing. You'd be interrogated when you went back to Ireland for the holidays –

Speaker Have you seen Bridie Murphy?

Fergal – as though England was a village and you'd get to know all in it. Everybody that arrived would be asked the same question and we'd all promise we'd keep our eyes peeled, we'd ask around for

Fergal/Speaker red haired Bridie Murphy

Fergal who walked out of the door one morning and not a word heard of since.

Aine Just hold it there, Da.

The DAT is not on. She cannot handle the machine because of the state of her floury hands.

Fergal She was the elder sister of one of our neighbours.

Aine Wait . . . (*She wipes her hands, rushing, nearly panicking, trying to clean them of flour.*)

Fergal Widowed young. Could've spent the rest of her time buried in the country – or just walk out of the door one morning without a backward glance.

Aine Da . . .

She handles the DAT, but is flustered, all fingers and thumbs.

Fergal The idea of it! The possibilities . . . To walk out that door . . . Where will you go? Who will you be this day?

Aine is in place with her equipment. We hear Maura and Seaneen, off.

Seaneen (*off*) Just get off my back, will you?

Maura (*off*) But Seaneen . . .

Aine (*encouragingly*) Go on . . .

Fergal looks at Aine as though seeing her for the first time. She holds the DAT out to him. He holds a mystified silence. Seaneen enters, pursued by Maura, who has a sheet from the line thrown over her shoulder. Fergal is immediately delighted to see him.

Fergal Son . . .

Seaneen takes in the scene, hovers, then walks straight through, exiting the other side. Maura stops still, a beat, looks at Aine, who guiltily holds the recording equipment.

Son?

A door slams, off. Aine switches off the offending DAT. A beat.

Maura He won't go. Twenty years we didn't have a parade. Over twenty years after the – (*inhalation*) – and him now calling me a nag –

Aine Everybody has the odd row. It's only human to arg –

Maura – We weren't. We don't. We have discussions. And he still won't go.

Aine Leave it, Mam.

Maura Twenty years we didn't have a parade. Over twenty years proving ourselves as decent human beings, good citizens, hard grafters. We pay our taxes. We pay the television licence. Your father never had a day off sick in his life. We never claimed dole, even when we had a right to it. We contributed. We built this city. We built this city but they never let us – always, when you least expect it – a gap in the sentence – as if we'd forget – a knowing look – haven't we paid our dues? We're decent people. And the one time I want to stand up in the public and be proud – the one time I want my family with me standing shoulder to shoulder – the one time I won't be ashamed – the one time – the one – and he won't – he – and it makes me – I'm feeling –

Fergal holds the match, looks at it, several beats.

Fergal Gutted.

He blows out the flame. Darkness.

End of sequence.

Two

Later in the afternoon.

Aine sits making notes from a video interview she has made with an older Irishwoman, rewinding/fast-forwarding the tape (signified by dots), searching for a particular anecdote. The screen should not be visible to the audience. The interviewee's voice is that of Speaker.

Speaker/Tape . . . Dancing at the crossroads all right, nothing else to do! (*laughter*) . . . England, England was . . .

Sound of prolonged fast-forwarding,. Aine is getting closer to what she wants.

. . . slammed the door in your face once they heard the accent. Oh, terrible, it was terr . . . woman at work, Maureen Connol . . . ransacked the house, even dug up the . . .

Satisfied, Aine rewinds to earlier in the story. She is absorbed, watching the video closely, making notes. Although initially recorded and from the video, the story is now performed live by Speaker, who enters the domestic space. The physical presence of Speaker is not apparent to Aine. Speaker stands beside Aine and even watches part of the video with her, continuing the speech as direct address, as during the opening. Most of Aine's responses are recorded, from the video machine.

Speaker/Live . . . Years ago, Maureen Connolly, one night out with friends, let slip her father used to be a member of the IRA. The old IRA, mind. At one point nearly every family in the thirty-two counties had an IRA sympathiser – end of story, or so Maureen thought, but what happened next sent the fear of God into her. Somewhere, somehow, along the lines Maureen's family 'secret' got into the ears of someone in authority. She was continuing her life quite blissfully when all of a sudden there was a knock at the door . . . Now, Aine, who do you think would come knocking on Maureen Connolly's door at three in the morning?

Aine/Tape (*faux-naive*) I don't know.

Speaker/Live Neither did Maureen. So imagine her surprise when it was the police.

Aine speaks aloud, a response to the story.

Aine/Live You're joking.

Speaker/Live I'm not. And neither were they. They ransacked the house, even dug up the garden, and why? Because there was some 'activity' here in Birmingham at the time and Maureen Connolly – whose forbears fought in the war of independence – was living here, so naturally, being an Irishwoman with that connection, she had to be guilty . . .

Aine/Tape What was it they were looking for?

Speaker/Live The usual. Guns. Explosives. Nuclear warhead. Sherman tank, I don't know – but of course, there was nothing. So they gave their apologies and left, with the house turned over and Maureen with a stammer she's kept to this very day. And this was in England, mind. In this very city.

Aine/Tape So what did she do?

Speaker/Live Have her husband put back the floorboards – and plant the garden with potatoes. Well, after it was dug up, they might as well make the most of it, ha? And a lovely crop they got – something to do with the thorough turning over of the soil.

Speaker starts making her way back out of the domestic setting – to a vantage point, slightly lower than for One.

She even thought of getting them back again, the following year. You know – send a postcard to Scotland Yard . . .

Aine calls out the punch-line, looking towards the window.

Aine The explosives are in the garden!

Billy is suddenly visible at the window, looking in. Aine is startled to see him, quickly switches off the video. He disappears. She crosses to the door stage right, half exits into the garden but is drawn back by the front-doorbell ringing. Leaving the kitchen door open, she exits stage left through the house. Billy reappears by the window, then sticks his head around the open kitchen door. He looks around for Fergal or Maura, enters edgily, notices Aine's notebook, can't help but look at what she's been writing. The front door slams. Aine re-enters perplexed, finds him staring down at her work. A beat.

Billy There's an ess in it.

Aine stares at him in astonishment. He points down to the page.

'IRA sympathiser' . . . Ess, not zed.

Aine immediately collects her work. Billy is nervy, but full of bravado, maybe the result of dutch courage.

Billy Your father about?

Aine What?

Billy Your Da.

Aine Yes. He's –

Billy They don't teach spelling by rote in the schools any more?

Aine No.

Billy It shows.
  So this is your work, then?

Aine Yes – oral history, reminiscence.

Billy What d'you actually do?

Aine I go round to the residential homes and –

Billy Is your mother home, Anne?

Aine I'm Aine, now.

Billy Ha?

Aine My name – Aine – it's Gaelic –

Billy Onion?

Aine Ain – doesn't matter. She isn't, no, home, that is.

Billy Don't they mind?

Aine Who?

Billy The old wans, being ripped off?

Aine What?!

Billy I don't suppose you have a root about in their knicker drawer for pearls, family heirlooms, whilst you're about it?

Aine I'm sorry?

Billy It's the biddies you should be apologising to, not me.

57

Aine Excuse me?

Billy You're very polite. For a thief.

Aine I'm a – !

Billy That's how I see it. Stealing.

Aine I . . .

Billy Father resting?

Aine After lunch, yes, he –

Billy Having part of yourself stolen. Your words.

Aine No, it's . . .

Billy Part of your life. Taken.

Aine It's . . .

Billy I'm with the Indians on this, y'know? Not allowing photographs; it steals part of the soul.

Aine We're validating their experiences.

Billy Them are big words for someone who can't spell.

Aine History. Where an Irish person begins and ends.

Billy So why are you doing it?

Aine We're compiling a library –

Billy You were born over here. I remember the night.

Aine – where people can study, do research . . .

Billy . . . Wouldn't you be better living your own life than poring over the small print of someone else's?

Aine stares at him. A beat.

Aine I'll tell my father you called. He'll be sorry he missed you.

Billy Ah, not at all. I'm in no hurry.

He goes to settle down in front of the TV/video.

D'you get the racing on that? I've a fiver on a knacker out of Leopardstown, three-thirty.

Aine I'm working.

He takes up the remote control and pats the seat beside him.

Billy Come on, now then, we'll be company for one another.

Aine I'm sorry but I really . . .

She takes the remote control back off him.

Billy Interview me, then, but there's no need to put 'the voice' on, I know you.

Aine I specialise in women immigrants.

Billy So do I. Lovely creatures. Nobody knows more about Biddy and Mary's movements than me. I'm an expert on it. Studied the fairer sex for the greater part of . . . (*He sees Aine's face.*) No?

Aine No. I have to get this done for tomorrow.

Billy The Parade?

Aine It's part of a community project. Information, a hand-out. Thirty years of the Birmingham-Irish . . .

Billy That's easy enough: spit, boom! Fiddle dee dee, 'charmed' . . .

Aine I'm a bit behind schedule, with Da and everything. So if you wouldn't mind . . .?

Billy Not at all, work away. I like a studious atmosphere.

He doesn't move from the seat. Aine hovers, at a loss.
A beat.

Aine Couldn't I get him to call you when he's up, or . . .

Billy Now, I'd like to accommodate you, Onion, but it's
a sensitive matter, of some urgency, so I'll wait for your
mother, if it's all the same with you. In the circumstances,
maybe she'd be the best to . . . (*He sees her expression.*)
Don't you be worrying your head. (*He takes out a*
newspaper and heads for the toilet.) I'll have a little sit
down in here, out of your way. It'll be *selon le vent* – as
the wind takes me. Don't wait up.

Billy exits into the toilet and closes the door. She tries
to work again but stops, frustrated, concentration
spoiled. She looks at her notes, tries to make sense of
them and finally throws them down. She goes to the
fridge for comfort, stands at the open door, looking
in. Seaneen enters stage right, carrying music store bags.

Seaneen Do you want a hand with your cases?
It's just – you've so obviously moved in again . . .

Aine . . . If you hadn't been out, gallivanting, I'd be
working in the peace of my own flat. You know Da can't
be left alone and –

Seaneen – Who rattled your cage?

Aine Billy fucking McFarland, if you must know, acting
like he owns the place.

Seaneen He's probably thinking about it – y'know,
making the oldies an offer they can't refuse. (*mimicking*)
'Mr Bricks and Mortar' trying the place out for size . . .

Aine He's test-driving the bog at the moment.

Seaneen I hope they're sensible and don't burn all their
bridges in case the 'wee little retirement cottage with

praities growing up the door' doesn't turn out to be quite
what they expect. They could be in for a nasty surprise.

Aine Do you exist in a parallel universe, or is it too
many Class A's making your brain go spongy?

Seaneen You what?

Aine Of course they're going to sell up – especially now,
with Da . . .

Scarcely a beat as they look at one another.

Seaneen They should go for a recky, first. It'll be a
mistake.

Aine Mam lives and breathes that place. It's her
inheritance. And ours, too.

Seaneen Sod that, just give me the money.

Aine She wants to die there.

Seaneen Well, that'll be easily arranged. They'll be
playing suicide games within a month for light
entertainment.

Aine It's their dream, all they've ever talked of for years.

Seaneen I've never heard Dad say –

Aine – Well you wouldn't, would you? I mean, you can't
spend one minute in the same room as him. You can't
hear him now, asking you to go to the parade tomor –

Seaneen – Do us a favour and change the fucking
record.

Aine Selective listening, I think it's called.

Seaneen (*overlapping*) He's only going on the bloody
march because Mom wants him to.

Aine (*overlapping*) You only hear what you want.

Seaneen And it's exactly the same with Ireland. He doesn't want to go back. Why leave everything you know and spend your retirement amongst strangers?

Aine Oh, I suppose you and he have been having lots of long chats about it, have you?

A beat. They stare at one another. Aine changes tack. Calmer.

It's always been their plan to go home. Once they get rid of the tenants on Mam's farm, they're moving back. Permanently.

Seaneen It'll be lethal, trying to go back to a place that only exists in the imagination. Mom's out of touch – in love with some romantic Ireland, trapped in a nineteen-fifties idyll, that probably didn't even exist then. In fact I know it didn't; Dad couldn't wait to leave the fucking place.

Aine That's not true.

Seaneen looks at her.

Even if it was in the past, it's different now.

Seaneen Well, Ireland certainly is, but do they know? The heroin capital of Europe, where a car is stolen every sixty seconds, fifty per cent of the population is under twenty and the proud holder of a suspect record for winning the Eurovision Song Contest too many times.

Aine Well, I'd go, given the opportunity.

Seaneen Aine, you've had the opportunity all your adult life and you've never gone, so what's so diff . . . Ah, Mammy and Daddy to hold your hand, support you whilst you retrain. Well, you'll have to. The 'diaspora industry' doesn't work inside Ireland, you'll lose your precious niche and that special title 'Professional Irishwoman'.

Aine I'd be a returnee.

Seaneen You were never there in the first place – assuming two weeks every Summer when we were kids doesn't count. It'd be same as it ever was: Irish in England, English in Ireland, and never the twain shall meet.

Aine I've got Irish citizenship.

Seaneen So does Jasmine Hussein who lives up the road. They'll give a green passport to any fucker if they think they're going to benefit.

Aine I identify myself as –

Seaneen – you were born and raised here.

Aine So? If a cat has kittens in an oven are they called biscuits? It doesn't matter where you're –

Billy's raised voice comes from behind the closed toilet door.

Billy (*off*) Of course it bloody does!

Billy, holding his trousers up in one hand, thrusts his head around the door.

It's there in the air you breathe, the events that shape you.

Aine But I've never fitted in here, I –

Billy The trouble with you young ones is having the luxury of time to think. *Mai fein*, the lot of yous. If you were out struggling to get a pot of spuds on the table to feed the family that evening, you wouldn't have time for worries about who you are and where you come from. Just be grateful you're not laying down in a ditch the side of the road with the hard rain on you. You're out of bog roll. Do you have a spare?

Seaneen throws him a roll of toilet paper. Billy withdraws again into the toilet. Seaneen is amused by

Billy's intervention, Aine is embarrassed. She gives Seaneen the finger. He laughs. She continues, lower in volume at first, mindful of Billy eavesdropping.

Aine I worry about you. Did you hatch out of a pod somewhere or get left on the doorstep? You can't be family – you're so unlike us. You don't seem to be connected to anything.

Seaneen Whereas you just tap into the centre of the cosmos . . .

Aine I feel part of something, yeah. Something outside me, bigger –

Seaneen (*interrupting*) – Careful, bab', or they'll be sending round a cult deprogrammer: 'Paddy brainwashed . . . the race that took over her mind . . . '

Aine Fuck off.

Seaneen Fuck off yourself.

Aine What are you going to do when Mam and Da have gone?

Seaneen Find a bedsit, I suppose. Might try Moseley or . . .

Aine . . . I meant when they die.

Seaneen Cheerful fucker, aren't you?

Aine It's going to happen.

Seaneen Later rather than sooner, I hope.

Aine But what'll you do then?

Seaneen Probably get a bedsit in (*Moseley*).

Aine Can't you be serious for once?

Seaneen (*thinks*) No.

Aine I worry about you.

Seaneen Don't.

Aine You'll have no idea of who you are or where you're from.

Seaneen I'm all right, me.

Aine You're not part of anything –

Seaneen Ever thought that might be by choice?

Aine You're going to vanish. Disappear off into the great beige blandness of what it is to be British.

Seaneen Beige bland . . . Where've you been living all your life? Birmingham.

Speaker In the belly of the beast.

Seaneen One of the most culturally diverse cities in Europe – the biggest racial mix in –

Aine (*interrupting*) Oh, enough of the public service broadcast, you know what I mean.

Seaneen I don't, actually.

Aine We're responsible for carrying the family line – and I don't mean just genes – but the memories, history, culture –

Seaneen Sod that. I'm a bit busy living at the moment – y'know, having experiences – making what will be my own past . . .?

Aine If you don't know where you've been, you don't know where you're going.

Seaneen Well, I know I've just been in HMV, so I must be on my way now to my bedroom and the CD player . . . (*He begins to leave.*)

Aine Seaneen . . .

Seaneen Why don't you call me Paddy or Mick and be done with it?

Aine I'm sorry, it's habit. It's your pet name.

Seaneen Well, maybe I'm no longer the pet. Maybe I've outgrown it.

Aine Maybe it's time you acted like an adult and maybe then we'd all get the message . . . Look at you – going into town to buy records on a Saturday, like we used to when we were kids and then mooning about in your bedroom listening to them, like a love-sick teenager. What, got your week's pocket money, have you? Pocket money from the government – or is Mam still subbing you?

Seaneen It's got nothing to do with you, what I choose to do with my life . . .

Aine No, not at all, even though you're becoming a walking stereotype. I mean, we all know now that Jesus Christ was really an Irishman. He didn't leave home until he was thirty-three. So you're all right – you've a few years, yet.

Seaneen Aine, just . . .

Seaneen turns, starts walking away. She calls after him.

Aine Dad's dying.

He stops, a pause.

He is, isn't he? He's going to die.

Another pause, without looking at her.

Seaneen We all are – some just get there quicker than others.

He starts exiting. She calls after him.

Aine You'll have to speak with Da some time or other. Sean – you'll regret it if you don't.

Seaneen has gone. Aine is at a loss, she picks up a book, puts it down, then wanders, as usual, to the fridge and the comforting ritual of gazing through its open door. She stands, looking. Maura enters stage right, with a pile of shopping bags she drops by the door. She makes eye contact with Aine, then goes back outside to collect more shopping. Aine takes the opportunity to exit stage left. Maura re-enters weighed down with booze, sees the bags still where she dropped them and no sign of Aine.

Maura What's new? All on my lonesome. I could win prizes in it.

She begins sorting through her packages – Irish whiskey and beer for St Patrick's – and a large plastic inflated shamrock which she puts with satisfaction on the side. The toilet door opens. Balling up his resolve, Billy is about to approach her when he stops and watches her unpacking and enjoying her dubious 'Oirish' memorabilia – an outsize 'Love me, I'm Irish' T-shirt, which she pulls on over her clothes – and a horrific stuffed leprechaun which, when pressed in the belly, says 'Begorrah'. Maura laughs, doing this several times, delighting in it, Billy softening as he watches. Finally she unpacks her treasure – a kitsch wind-up music box, in the shape of a thatched cottage. She sets it going and it plays 'I'll Take You Home Again, Kathleen'. She listens, swaying to the tune. Billy, strengthening his resolve, is about to speak to her when Fergal enters, drawn to the music. Frustrated and still unseen, Billy withdraws back into the toilet, grabbing a bottle of the hard stuff for company. Maura, oblivious, speaks.

67

Maura When I grow up, I'm going to be Queen of England. Queen of England with the diamonds and the tiaras and they'll all have to bow and scrape down to me.

Fergal (*joining her*) Isn't Queen of Dublin City enough for you, then?

There is sense of a memory, them reliving a moment – we glimpse in them the young Maura and Fergal from the past as the music box plays.

Maura And I'll drive by in the carriage preening and waving and all the riff-raff would shield their eyes from the beauty.

Fergal Amn't I blinded already?

Maura And all them oul bitches will gawp and stare at Maura Canally as was, coming to this.

Fergal Which of the oul bitches?

Maura The oul bitches at home.

Fergal At home? Maura, aren't we there already?

They stare out, him with satisfaction, at another room, held in their mind's eye.

It'll be a little palace with a lick of paint. And maybe you'll put some curtains at the windows?

Maura I will indeed. The house opposite is that close you could lean out of the window and shake hands, if they had it in them to be friendly. So close you can smell it when they fart.

Fergal So I'll grow flowers in the window-box and protect the royal nose.

Maura My mother always said I was too particular.

Fergal No, just – fussy.

Maura We'll have to be particular if we want to get on. Decent. Good neighbours. It's a new start, Fergal. We can make ourselves be whatever we want.

The music box, which has been slowing down, stops. The moment is gone .

D'you remember? The little flat over the butcher shop in Oldbury with the sloped roof and cracked pane of glass in the skylight over the bed. How I hated it. The smell. After the country, I thought I'd die for a lung-full of air. And you promised me we wouldn't be here long, just make our fortunes and get the hell back to Ireland, to have our children and maybe a clutch of chickens, raise both of them at home, free range. Fergal, do you . . . (*remember*)?

Fergal I'm sorry. Should I . . .?

Maura No, no, not at all. No matter. It was all a long time ago.

End of sequence.

Three

*Aine sits before the video, making notes and looking up
references in a book on the Irish diaspora. Maura sits
sewing, altering her shop-bought clothes, as opening. She
still wears her out-sized T-shirt. Fergal sits in his chair,
apparently asleep, the matchstick farmhouse beside him.
It is more complete than previously. The Speaker is
visible, actively observing. She has a different vantage
point, closer to the action. Descending. Maura tries on
the garment, checking her sewing. She resumes sewing.
Throughout, the video plays quietly and continuously,
the text in brackets going beneath Aine and Maura's
dialogue. Woman's voice on the tape is that of the
Speaker. Asterisks indicate points of overlap.*

Woman on Tape A great haemorrhage of people from
the land. Whole communities withered. It was as if their
very roots had been ripped up, thrown away. Villages
became ghost towns. *

  Maura's overlapping dialogue begins.

(Only the very old or infirm remained in what had once
been thriving communities. Houses were left to fall in on
themselves as the young migrated, chasing work or
escaping the church.)

Maura (*overlapping*) * Jesus, Aine, haven't you something
that's a little less depressing?

Aine I'm trying to get this thing done for tomorrow –

Maura It's supposed to be a festival, a celebration.
You'll have people slitting their wrists.

Aine hushes her. Silence, except for the recording.

Woman on Tape People would follow one another.
I heard of whole communities recreating themselves the
other side of the world! An aunt'd go to Boston, her
niece'd follow . . . It made a pattern, like the geese flying
in Autumn. *

*Maura interrupts again, Aine ignores her. Tape
continues, low.*

(You'd already feel connected to a place through a line of
those who went before. It was like a trail was established,
a route which became well trodden. And there's no part
of the world where the Irish hasn't settled: England,
America, Australia – all over. A presence on every
continent – good workers as well as good spenders –
welcomed everywhere – with the odd exception. And
that's where I made a mistake. I should've thought more
about where to go instead of just following the crowd.)

Maura * I think she's talking through her hat. Some
were pioneers, went by themselves. There was a woman
there from home, just upped and went. Gone. I always
wondered what happened to her. Bridie Murphy. Just –
disappeared off the face of the earth.

*She contemplates the video, Aine is hunched,
concentrated.*

Aine – how do you choose who you interview? I mean . . .
what if it's a load of old nonsense . . .?

Aine What?!

Maura Nothing – no – pay no attention, sorry I
interrupted.

*Aine goes back to her video, Maura continues with
her sewing. Woman on Tape continues in the
background.*

Woman on Tape My elder sister was doing all right for herself, so she sent for me. *

Overlapping begins, the recording continues, below dialogue.

(Instead of heading for where I really wanted to go, I got on the boat and landed up in Liverpool. It was just a train ride then to the Midlands and the typing pool. My sister had lined me up a job in Longbridge. The money was all right and they told me it was a start, so I went and that was my mistake.)

* *A burst of loud music, off.*

Maura He'll wake your father.

Aine leaps up, remote control in hand, opens the door to the house and yells up the stairs.

Aine (*shouts*) Sean!

Seaneen (*off*) Wha'?

Aine Mam says will you lower that racket before you wake Da?

Seaneen (*off*) I can't hear you?

Aine (*shouting, exiting*) Mam says . . .

Maura Mother of God – that's enough to wake the dead between yous.

Maura pushes over the door, glances with concern over at Fergal, who shifts, but then settles. There is sudden silence, but for the tape. We clearly hear the following.

Woman on Tape Yes, that was my mistake. I would've been better off in America. They love us over there – always wantin' you to sing or tell a story – party piece, y'know – but in England . . .?

Maura I lived it; I don't have to listen to it.

Speaker and recorded voice speak in unison as Maura hunts for the video remote control. She picks one up – the TV remote – tries it, it doesn't work. She continues searching as:

Speaker/Tape You had to keep your head down.

Maura Lying awake every night –

Woman on Tape They never liked us –

Maura – dreaming of a childhood in Ireland –

Speaker – always treated us with suspicion.

Maura – wishing I'd never . . .

Maura is unaware of Aine standing at the door, remote in hand, watching. Speaker watches her watching.

Woman on Tape And after they brought in the Prevention of Terrorism Act, well that was it, really.

Maura The usual pattern. Have children, be tied to the Church, decent.

Woman on Tape You'd be arrested for blowing your nose.

Maura Knitting the kids' Arans, buying them the best quality clothes and sending them to drama class to avoid any kind of accent.

Aine Why no accent?

Startled, Maura stands still. She listens.

Woman on Tape I read thousands were detained, only a handful charged. You wouldn't know why they were holding you in solitary – and they didn't have to tell you – just leave you to rot.

Aine Why didn't you want me to have a voice like yours?

Maura is still, listening, Woman's voice speaks.

Woman on Tape But the worst thing was the Birmingham Six. Sent a chill through you, taught you to behave.

Speaker If it could happen to them, then why not you?

Maura suddenly unplugs the video. A moment's silence. She takes the video remote control off Aine, clutches her sewing.

Maura I should've saved me money. I spent a fortune on elocution lessons. Wanted youse to sound like you'd come from nowhere and your brother's a Brummie and you sound like you've just got off the boat.

Aine I had to invent it.

Maura That sounds about right.

Aine Thanks.

They look at each other.

Why wouldn't you let me be like you?

Maura busies herself with her sewing.

Maura Don't you ever listen to what's on them tapes, or is it in one ear and out the other?

Aine (*not without irony*) I'd like to hear it from the original source.

A beat.

Maura After the – after the (*inhalation*) – there was bad feeling.

Aine (*overlapping*) After the what, Mam?

Maura It wasn't safe. I wanted you to get on and do well and have all the opportunities I didn't. It was better

to be English. After the (*inhalation*) it was better to
sound like you came from nowhere.

Aine (*overlapping*) The what?

Maura Oh, everybody wants to be Irish, now, but there
was a time when the accent could lose you a job or get
you a glass in the face.

Aine You can't say it, can you? After the . . . You can't
even say it.

> *Maura tries on the garment she's been altering.*
> *It doesn't fit, she starts tearing at the stitches.*
> *Unacknowledged, Speaker moves from her vantage*
> *point into the room.*

Maura I can never get anything to fit in this place.

Aine No one will talk about the pub bombings.
They shaped me.

Maura They did, did they? Shape you? And what about
me? Don't you think they 'shaped' me? And the
thousands affected – never mind those poor ones that
were bereaved?

> *Speaker's proximity to Maura (perhaps a touch on the*
> *shoulder) creates an immediate outpouring of what*
> *has been unvoiced for so long.*

It's a scar. Oh, some clever clogs think it's well healed
over and able to be talked about – 'documented' – but
no. You want to hear of our shame.

Aine I didn't mean to –

Maura (*interrupting*) You want to put your fingers in
the wound and hear our cry. It lasts. It lingers.

Aine It was over twenty-four years ago . . .

Maura So? D'you think that makes any difference? Do
you really think time and distance cures anything? So put

your tape on – get your precious recording equipment out and I'll tell you – I'll tell you about the heart being blown out of the city we helped build. I'll tell you what it was like to be spat at in the street, having names hurled after you if you so much as opened your mouth and they heard the accent. Made guilty by association. They tried to lynch a fella at the car factory where your father worked. Got out the rope and everything: 'String up the Mick.' And you know something? I didn't blame them. The crime was so terrible, every Irish person felt shame. We didn't want to be part of that. Some of us had emigrated to escape that trouble and here it was, following us. So to do penance, good Catholics that we were, we got rid of all signs of our pride in where we came from – *mea culpa, mea culpa, mea maxima culpa* – we put everything underground and spent the better part of our lives being ambassadors – showing we were trustworthy, law-abiding, *decent* – but when any other atrocity happened, we were back on the front-line of blame. And we didn't want our children to suffer the same.

She begins collecting Aine's videos and books.

So now here we are in so-called peacetime, with your courses and your books and 'Irish Studies' when it's something I lived – but I'm not interested in being part of your curriculum.

Maura starts piling the resource material into her daughter's arms.

I'm not interested in being one of your case histories. I just want to go home. I've always hated this city. I don't want to be in this country. I've counted the days we were here, desperate to get back where I belong. And I'm going. But first I'm going to walk through this city with my head held high. And if anyone shouts at me to get off the road, I'll tell them your father built the road; that we own the fucking road.

Maura, looking determined, exits on a mission, Speaker takes a different vantage point. Aine, astonished, remains motionless, arms filled with books, where she stands. Several beats. Seaneen wanders through to the fridge, opens it, speaks as he looks in.

Seaneen What is it with you and that stuff? Are you really such a lightweight, Anne? Frightened you'll float away unless you've got your history to pin you down?

Aine It's important.

Seaneen I can't see how. Ordinary people leading ordinary lives.

Aine It needs to be remembered.

Seaneen Why?

Aine Because otherwise we'll lose it. All these voices, stories . . .

Seaneen . . . all trapped in some video library which'll never see the light of day again. D'you really think there's a future in this diaspora oral history thing? What? Put them all on the internet – cyber-mammy who'll tell you about the racist anti-Irish laws and how we suffered but never had our spirits broken? You have to move on and let go. That's progress.

Aine We need to know –

Seaneen – nothing. Because we don't live in the future or the past, but here. Now.

Aine opens her arms. Her resource material spills onto the floor. She exits, following Maura. Fergal sits, eyes shut, Seaneen stands passively looking into the fridge,

*studying the contents for some time. Suddenly he
becomes aware of Fergal's quiet presence. It is
unsettling. He looks over, tries to ignore his unease,
looks back into the fridge, the feeling persists. He has
to speak.*

Seaneen You all right, Dad?

*No answer. Several beats. Seaneen approaches him
warily. Fergal is still, eyes closed. Seaneen stops, a
slow panic building. He moves forward again. Fergal
speaks.*

Fergal Shocking business, pain.

Seaneen Dad?

Fergal opens his eyes and looks at Seaneen.

Fergal Learning to breathe in a new atmosphere.

A beat.

Did you ever know me? Did you ever know Fergal
Rourke?

*Deeply affected, Seaneen begins backing away, hands
held up – no more. Father and son study each other
from a distance.*

You're the next, now. There's no escaping.

*A long, uncomfortable silence.
The toilet flushes.
A beat. There is muffled laughter from within, then
Billy emerges, the worse for wear, falling backwards
through the door.*

Billy Thirty fucking years – and what's there to show
for it? Three decades working the roads and I haven't
even me signature on Spaghetti Junction. That's a great
Irish work, forget fucking *Ulysses*. We left not a trace,

all used aliases – a different name each place, to avoid
paying stamp. I was W.B. Yeats in Liverpool, Ian Paisley
in Nuneaton, Eamonn de Valera in the Black Country.
A whole gang of us could've been Pope Pius the Innocent
and they wouldn't have batted an eyelid, so long as they
had a name on the form. They didn't know what side
you were from and they didn't care – Protestant,
Catholic, bollox – for good or for ill, we were all Paddy.

*Maura re-enters with a large box still in Christmas
wrapping paper. It is a present from the previous
Christmas, opened, but not used. Aine, trailing
inquisitively in her wake, is immediately engaged by
Billy. Maura unwraps her present, revealing a karaoke
machine which she begins to assemble, via her
television and video. She is engrossed, ignoring Billy,
who continues his story undeterred, taking the floor.*

They'd pick us up at the side of the road – standing there
like goms at six-thirty in the morning – desperate for the
work, like – and if you'd been a bit weak of late, or
recovering from the sickness, you'd be shucked down
into the donkey jacket, hiding behind the lads, your
boots full of muck and on display – proving you were a
worker – and hoping the boss wouldn't see the pigeon
chest or hear the cough.
    Then into the back of the van if you were picked –
some big thick acting like a Roman emperor – thumbs
down and it's nothing to send home to the mother that
week – thumbs up and it's pints and chasers, into the
back of the Bedford van sharp, boys, fighting over who'd
have the shite seat over the wheel-arch and you'd be off,
driving with these cowboys into Christ knows what
sunrise – not sure what the job'd be – digging the road,
laying pipes – not knowing if you'd be back in one piece.
    I've seen grown men melted to lard when the pick axe
cut through the mains. Another drowned on concrete.

A fourth fell through the monkey-run and broke his back. Val Doonican on his way to hospital, Padraig Pearse lying silent in the morgue and not one of them insured, not one of them protected and none of us knowing their real names, nor next-of-kin address.

And d'you know something? It was fucking great, I fucking loved it, but what have I now? What do I own?

Aine (*moved*) Your stories. Culture.

Seaneen Fuck right off. As if a story'd clothe and feed him.

Billy Right.

Seaneen You can't cuddle up to your culture for warmth on a freezing night, can you, Billy?

Seaneen and Billy bonding, standing shoulder to shoulder, sharing the remains of the whiskey bottle, arms about one another.

Billy No.

Seaneen It doesn't bring you a cup of tea in the morning, does it, Billy boy? Or stand you a pint at the bar, or tell you it loves you?

Billy No, you're right, you're fucking right, son.

Seaneen is beginning to wind Billy up to a pitch. Aine walks away with dignity. Maura tries the karaoke machine.

Maura (*through mic*) One two, one two.

She presses a button and a loud crash of simulated orchestral music blares out. She changes it to Country and Western. There is a short introduction then Maura, Billy and Seaneen launch into a Country and Irish rendition of 'Stand by your Man'.

All
    Sometimes it's hard to be a woman,
    Giving all your love to just one man . . .

*The lights go down on the singers and up on Aine and
Fergal, who has laboured breathing.*

Fergal The air was different, once we were headed for
that boat. A whole generation shipping out, not knowing
where we were headed nor what would become of us
and not too curious, either. Would it have been trust?

Aine I don't know.

Fergal The laws of life, the way things worked changed –
and before I knew it, I was trying to become someone
else.

Speaker A navvy, a frequenter of public houses, a cheat,
one who cut corners in work. Once, he could leap a five-
bar gate, coax a hen into laying, cure colic and ringworm,
tell a bird by its singing. Once, he could raise the roof of
a house with his playing, the heels drumming across the
stone floor, the laughter loud and willing. He became an
adulterer, a cynic, a non-churchgoer, one who spat in the
street. He looked brazenly at women's legs and brazenly
asked if he could follow them home. He kissed hard, he
cried after, cursed his mother, prayed to Our Lady.

Fergal It was a whole brand new world.

Speaker With the tag still on it.

Fergal And I owned it. I could afford anything.

Speaker Knew the price of everything and the value of
nothing, walked with a swagger, talked with his fists,
inspired fear and bred hatred, remembered feast days,
gave as good as he was given, said love words when he
didn't mean it, never said love words when he felt it.

Fergal We were the men. The men. Rooted so deep in the old soil, we could change our husbandry, plant something new.

Speaker The solace of myth-making.

Fergal But no. There's no escaping.

Back to normal, through the microphone the bellow of:

Seaneen Stand by your Mam . . . (*Seaneen puts on a ridiculous Country and Western accent.*) Thank you, thank you. I'd just like to share something with y'all now . . . My thanks, my gratitude to the woman who gave me life . . . My own, the one and only . . . Ma . . .

Maura moves stiffly out of Seaneen's embrace.

Maura Don't you be thinking I'll forget about the Parade. I haven't forgiven you that, yet.

Seaneen I can't see the logic in celebrating what's basically an accident of birth.

Maura (*to Fergal*) D'you hear your son here talking?

Upset, Maura moves away, begins fussing in the kitchen, making sandwiches that no one will eat. Fergal continues making his kit. Billy tries to intervene, but Seaneen blatantly ignores him.

Billy Look – I've an excuse for not liking marching parades – a certain association with events from where I come from – but I'd fucking go, just to please them. D'ye hear what I'm saying, now?

Seaneen What's St Pat's? A load of people going out on the piss regardless of their nationality, and, if they're lucky, not going home in an ambulance.

Maura The Parade's not like that. That's not what it's about.

Billy Just go to the Parade for fuck's sake – it's an afternoon out of your life – a couple of shagging hours. Don't live to regret this, lad – do it for your Da.

Seaneen St Patrick: patron saint of cirrhosis of the liver.

Aine You just have to belittle everything.

Seaneen Oh, do us all a favour and lighten up. You've the face of a smacked arse.

Aine Don't insult me, our parents, their friends and things that are important.

Seaneen (*speaking over her*) I never knew doing history required the surgical removal of your sense of humour.

Aine When you know what's happened in the past – the hardships, struggles, even what these people put up with, you'd see there's every reason to celebrate, every reason to . . .

Seaneen (*speaking over her*) Who gives a shit? It's gone, past. Hello! Twenty-first century . . . Travel light.

Aine What are you scared of, Seaneen? That you won't be able to hack it, not man enough to handle the load?

Seaneen I'm not interested and I'm tired of this crap. It's like a religion; stop trying to convert me.

Aine Seaneen, that's –

Seaneen – I don't need to carry a memorial to the dead on my back to make me feel alive.

Aine strikes him. Shocked, they look at one another, then stand apart. Maura quits her mound of sandwiches, puts her hand up the chimney and pulls down the box of Irish cigarettes. She lights the remaining four cigarettes, handing Aine and Seaneen one each. She keeps one and gives the fourth to Billy,

who joins them. They stand in a row, smoking in
silence. Long, long pause filled with silent, studious
smoking. The dynamic changes. Eventually they
simultaneously extinguish the cigarettes.

Billy (*to Maura*) . . . I'm bankrupt.
I've lost everything.
The business is bust.
All with receivers.
I didn't know how to tell you. I've been waiting all
day, trying to –

Maura Is there anything we can do?

Billy Forgive me.

Maura Billy, that juice has gone to your brains.

Billy I lost all that was invested in me.

Maura Aine, put some coffee on.

Aine does so, busying herself with the task.

Billy Every penny is gone.

Maura I promise you, it won't be as bad as it seems.

Billy Maura –

Maura It's always the darkest hour before the dawn.

Billy You don't understand.

Maura And you'll find some money from somewhere
and pay back them you owe.

Billy From where? I don't even have me bus fare.

Maura Something'll turn up.

Billy I'm retirement age and I won't even get the state
pension. I never paid National Insurance – I was
convinced I'd go home.

Maura Where's the crime in that? Fergal and I have the same plan . . .

Billy But Maura . . .

Maura . . . and they're begging now for us to return. The economy's grand. It'd be a good time –

Billy There's nothing to return to.

Maura We'd put you up, until you're steady.

Billy It's gone, Maura.

Maura And I could do with a hand around the place.

Billy The farmhouse. Your farmhouse. It's gone.

Maura My –

Billy Gone.
I'm sorry, Maura.

She stops. All listen, only Fergal hearing Speaker's contribution. Maura stands staring at Fergal, as does Speaker.

You know how things were there for a good while. Irish land wasn't worth dirt. All the money was in England. Rebuilding. Construction. Our lads out on the sites. The old homestead could collapse in on itself for all anyone cared –

Speaker – and some would dance in the ruins and trample the earth down, for good measure.

Billy Ireland was, it was . . .

Fergal . . . like living in a coffin.

Billy . . . distant. You had the kids and they were Brummies.
Fergal said you were here to stay.

Speaker Why go back in your old age to a place filled with ghosts?

Billy Better to use the house as an investment; get a good return.
   So we used it as collateral.

Maura No – we were renting it out. You know that more than anyone – you were handling –

Billy (*interrupting*) We used it as collateral to get a loan from the bank, then put the money into my business.

Maura But I didn't (*agree*) . . .

Billy It was in his name. When you married, you signed the house over to Fergal.
   It was a good investment, a sure thing.
   We didn't know how things would turn out.
   It was grand, for years.
   We never knew the business would go bust and the bank'd claim the house.
   We didn't –
   I'm sorry.
   Maura, I'm –

Maura breaks her stare from Fergal and exits.

End of sequence.

Four

Later, debris.

Distraught calm.

The karaoke machine is on, synthesised background sentimental Irish music. The TV screen is facing the audience, where the lyrics of the songs are displayed. A bouncing ball goes along the words to 'If You Ever Go Across the Sea to Ireland' and 'Danny Boy'. Aine sits on the floor beside the karaoke machine, her Irish-interest books, empty beer cans and the whiskey bottle scattered about her. Maura is absent. Billy lies on his back in a corner, apparently sleeping or passed out. Seaneen plays with the 'oirish' memorabilia, at moments setting up a double act between him and the leprechaun. Fergal sits by the completed matchstick farmhouse. Speaker is not present. Aine speaks through the microphone, her voice distorted, quoting from 'Yearning: Race, Culture and Gender' by bell hook .

Aine (*mic*) 'For those with no places that can safely be called 'home', there must be a struggle for a place to be.'

Seaneen presses the speaking leprechaun's belly.

Leprechaun Begorrah.

Aine I've never felt comfortable here. I'm not like you. I've never fitted in. Since I was a kid 'home' has been elsewhere, some place other than where I live.

He presses the speaking leprechaun's stomach.

Leprechaun Begorrah.

Aine I wanted authenticity.
I wanted to go back, but I was never there.

Seaneen You've been trying too hard.

Leprechaun Begorrah.

She throws the book down to the side.

Aine I have the parentage, citizenship – bank account.
I know my history, culture – I'm even learning the bloody
language – but I'm still Plastic Paddy, hand-crafted in
Digbeth.

*Maura enters. She is holding herself together, brittle,
sharp. She is oblivious to Seaneen and Aine and
acutely aware of Fergal, but refusing to even look
in his direction. He sits, passive, in the chair. Her
children are absorbed, unaware of her presence.*

Seaneen *(to Aine)* You know, I used to really want to
be like you. I tried learning all the dates, the famous
martyrs, like you. But then I realised it's someone else's
experience and I want to live my own.

Aine But it's still important.

Seaneen Why?

Aine People died.

Seaneen Big deal. They do that every day. Death is easy.
It's the living bit that's hard.

Fergal *(quietly)* Did you ever know me? Did you ever
know Fergal Rourke?

*Maura goes to the kitchen area, finding herself
surrounded by the spoiled soda bread, Kimberley
biscuits, unfinished breakfast and mound of untouched
sandwiches – signs of her domestic rituals, now
fragmented, disrupted. As in One, she grips the sink,
holds on, it passes.*

Maura (*barely audible*) It was lies. All lies.

Seaneen The past's full of pain and complaints and hatred and desires for revenge. It's bloody dangerous. Bury it, I say.

Leprechaun Begorrah.

Seaneen And throw in nationalism whilst you're about it, too. (*He throws the toy away from him.*) All I know is when people look at their history and get uppity about who they are, part of where they live gets annexed.

Aine You talk such bollox.

Seaneen I use the internet, right? And I chat with people from all over the world – kids from Mostar, Berlin, Gaza . . . We've watched the boundaries being redrawn so many times, we're not interested in them.
  Bury the past. Let it go.

Maura examines the palms of her hands, her speech is simultaneous and continues under the following.

Maura (*quiet intensity*) . . . Dennehys . . . the Widow Cross . . .

Fergal (*whispered*) Did you? Did you know – ?

Seaneen If we don't, we'll be taking revenge – or doing penance – or trying to atone for someone else's actions the rest of our lives.

Maura . . . Hanratty's . . . my father's field, my father's . . .

Seaneen Something that happened two centuries ago has nothing to do with me, now. Why Black 47 and not Rwanda, Kosovo or some other bloody massacre? Why one part of the world and not the rest?

Aine Because it's ours.

Seaneen I don't want it.

Maura suddenly clenches her hands into fists.

Maura (*barely audible*) Bury the past. Bury it. Bury,
bury, bury it deep in the good soil.

*Fergal begins speaking in a pattern similar to
Speaker's opening speech.*

Fergal When he was born in England –

Seaneen I'm not Irish, English –

Fergal – not the land of his fathers –

Seaneen I'm European –

Fergal – he was Seaneen, still son of the sons of the
Rourke clan . . .

Seaneen A citizen of the world!

Fergal You're next, son. There's no escaping.

Seaneen I don't want it. I don't want to be owned or
claimed.
  Like being in a corpse's shroud – sewn up both sides.
  I want to make it up for myself.

Aine I've nothing else to hold on to. Give me an
alternative and I'll consider it.

Fergal I never thought then it could kill you.

*Aine looks about the room for other alternatives. She
takes in Billy, her brother, her mother, her father.*

Maura That's it, I'm getting my coat.

*Maura marches across to her coat. No one tries to
stop her. She puts the coat on, but is unable to move.
She has nowhere else to go. She stands.*

Aine I've just seen the family resemblance.
  We all dream with our eyes open and we're all fucking
fakes.

A beat.

Maura We're not going, are we Fergal?
Not going home.

Fergal Home?
Aren't we there already?

The lights dim as Fergal sets the matchstick farmhouse alight. It burns. He acknowledges the audience and leaves the stage.

The farmhouse burns.

End of sequence.

Coda

Late in the morning. 17 March. St Patrick's Day.

The room is dark and full of the debris from the night before.

Aine enters from the stairs, crosses and pulls back the curtains on the window. Immediately Maura is visible, sitting in the chair, her coat still on, the Irish T-shirt underneath. It should be clear she has been here all night, holding on to herself.

The burnt-out matchstick farmhouse is nearby.

Aine goes to touch Maura, for her own comfort as much as her mother's, but is unable to. Maura rejects all physical contact.

Aine stands, useless, bereft, not knowing what to do, and then out of routine opens the fridge and looks in, finds no comfort there, crosses and puts the kettle on for tea.

After several beats, Billy appears at the window, looks in, then enters at the door. He is groomed, hair slicked down, dressed in a long dark overcoat. Silence. Seaneen then joins him, entering from outside, dressed sombrely and unusually formal. Moments pass.

Maura You've booked the arrangements?

Seaneen nods.

And for after the service?

Again, the nod.

Booked the tickets?

Seaneen Three return and one . . . One . . .

He cannot say it, Billy says it for him.

Billy One repatriation cargo.

They absorb this information.

Maura That's it, then.

*Several beats. All stand, emotionally frozen.
Billy twitches, has to speak.*

Billy But Maura – don't you think he'd have preferred
to –

*She silences him with a look. He wavers, but has to
say.*

Billy I mean – Birmingham was always his –

Maura – He's going home.

*They stand, unsure what to do. Several beats.
Into the silence comes the distant sound of music
and people marching. All are still, listening. It comes
closer, the St Patrick's Day Parade. Acute, they listen
and mentally observe it as it grows louder then fades,
passing the house. This should take some time. As the
sounds of the Parade pass and fade away, so do the
energies of the mourners, excepting Maura, who is
steely-eyed and erect in her mourning, and Seaneen
who, terribly, stares ahead. Eventually he, too, moves
away to the peripheries.
Maura stands.
The Speaker appears at her vantage point. As she
speaks, there is a slow fade on the domestic setting.*

Speaker Bridie Murphy – who remembered the feast
days alongside the Irish martyrs, who made the warmest
Aran, the sweetest, most thirst-quenching tea, whose
hands were broad and capable, fashioned for carrying
eggs and soothing children. Bridie, who walked out of

the house one morning in her sister's second-best dress
and the egg money from the yellow jug on the dresser
sewn into the lining of her jacket, bound for America.
Bridie, who left without telling.

Bridie, who had not been heard of since.

Bridie, who was found two weeks after death in a
rented room in Queen's; who bagged a millionaire in
Florida. Bridie, who gave up the bacon and cabbage and
crying over Mother Ireland and who leads the life of
Reilly. Bridie, who metamorphosed into a knacker on the
Kilburn High Road, asking you to sing 'I'll Take You
Home Again, Kathleen', pawing at your shirt, tears in
her eyes.

Bridie who has passed into myth.

Bridie, who haunts dreams, embodies shadows flitting
on the night-time ceiling. Bridie who is the banshee of
the diaspora, tapping at the window, wailing for the next
to disembark. Bridie who is everyone and nowhere.

Bridie – who has the adventures of Ulysses . . .

Lights fade on Speaker.

End.

Discover the brightest and best in fresh theatre writing
with Faber's new StageScripts

Sweetheart by Nick Grosso (0571 17967 3)
Mules by Winsome Pinnock (0571 19022 7)
The Wolves by Michael Punter (0571 19302 1)
Gabriel by Moira Buffini (0571 19327 7)
Skeleton by Tanika Gupta (0571 19339 0)
The Cub by Stephanie McKnight (0571 19381 1)
Fair Game by Rebecca Prichard (0571 19476 1)
(a free adaptation of **Games in the Backyard** by Edna Mazya)
Crazyhorse by Parv Bancil (0571 19477 x)
Sabina! by Chris Dolan (0571 19590 3)
I Am Yours by Judith Thompson (0571 19612 8)
Been So Long by Che Walker (0571 19650 0)
Yard Gal by Rebecca Prichard (0571 19591 1)
Sea Urchins by Sharman Macdonald (0571 19695 0)
Twins by Maureen Lawrence (0571 20065 6)
Skinned by Abi Morgan (0571 20007 9)
Real Classy Affair by Nick Grosso (0571 19592 x)
Down Red Lane by Kate Dean (0571 20070 2)
Shang-a-Lang by Catherine Johnson (0571 20077 x)
The Storm by Alexander Ostrovsky
trs. Frank McGuinness (0571 20004 4)
By Many Wounds by Zinnie Harris (0571 20097 4)
So Special by Kevin Hood (0571 20044 3)
The Glory of Living by Rebecca Gilman (0571 20140 7)
Certain Young Men by Peter Gill (0571 20191 1)
Paddy Irishman, Paddy Englishman and Paddy . . . ?
by Declan Croghan (0571 20128 8)
Pelleas and Melisande by Maurice Maeterlinck
trs. Timberlake Wertenbaker (0571 20201 2)
Martha, Josie and the Chinese Elvis
by Charlotte Jones (0571 20237 3)
Dogs Barking by Richard Zajdlic (0571 20006 0)
All That Trouble That We Had by Paul Lucas (0571 20267 5)
The Bedsit by Paul Sellar (0571 20364 7)
Drink, Dance, Laugh and Lie by Samuel Adamson (0571 20442 2)
The Map Maker's Sorrow by Chris Lee (0571 20365 5)
Silence by Moira Buffini (0571 20445 7)
Bitter with a Twist by Simon Treves (0571 20479 1)
My Dad's Corner Shop by Ray Grewal (0571 20534 8)
Jump Mr Malinoff, Jump by Toby Whithouse (0571 20584 4)
The Waiting Room by Tanika Gupta (0571 20514 3)
Still Time by Stephanie McKnight (0571 20782 0)
The Slight Witch by Paul Lucas (0571 20935 1)
Behind the Scenes at the Museum by Bryony Lavery (0571 20911 4)
A Wedding Story by Bryony Lavery (0571 20906 8)
Belonging by Kaite O'Reilly (0571 20902 5)